ANOTHER NUN'S STORY

An Impossible Dream

B E T H   W A R R E N

WESTBOW
P R E S S®
A DIVISION OF THOMAS NELSON
& ZONDERVAN

This book is a work of non-fiction. Unless otherwise noted, the author and the publisher make no explicit guarantees as to the accuracy of the information contained in this book and in some cases, names of people and places have been altered to protect their privacy.

WestBow Press books may be ordered through booksellers or by contacting:

WestBow Press
A Division of Thomas Nelson & Zondervan
1663 Liberty Drive
Bloomington, IN 47403
www.westbowpress.com
844-714-3454

ISBN: 978-1-6642-2678-4 (sc)
ISBN: 978-1-6642-2677-7 (hc)
ISBN: 978-1-6642-2679-1 (e)

Library of Congress Control Number: 2021904554

Print information available on the last page.

WestBow Press rev. date: 05/04/2021

Contents

**To my parents
who always helped me
make my dreams possible**

Acknowledgements

This book would have never come to fruition without the assistance of my friend, Beth Lehn, who has been my "guiding star." Editing, proofreading, computer support, consultation, encouragement, and **patience**, were her gifts to me during my writing process. I could never fully express my gratitude to Beth for her generosity in helping to make this book possible.

I am also indebted to my family and other friends who provided practical and motivational support for me. Shirley Bower, Jaime Lazarus, Joe McNulty, Patricia McNulty, and Jane Moody have generously assisted me with their strong proof-reading skills, and their problem-solving expertise, especially for those wicked computer issues.

Without the input of my family and friends, this book would still be in its early stages—in my file.

Introduction

Another **Nun's Story** is a memoir of my joys and difficulties during my religious life from the 1940s to the 1980s. This was an era when nuns were totally dependent on superiors for their welfare.

I tried to be a "good nun," but I was always attempting to be the person someone else expected me to be. I finally realized that the only One whose expectations really mattered was God. He never asked me to change my persona. He loves me just the way I am.

I entered the convent because I believed God was calling me to a special life of service for His people. I had a passionate love for nuns who combined their religious lives with outgoing compassion for others. I wanted to be just like them. I dreamed that answering my Call to religious life would help me make the world a better place.

In the beginning, I loved religious life and my Sisters. As far as I was concerned, I had found a beautiful family of loving and generous women. Receiving my religious name and accepting my Holy Habit were some of the greatest joys I have ever experienced.

Just as in other Communities, our superiors trained us in the "Community way of life." It was their duty to shape us in ways they perceived to be the most acceptable to God. They taught us just as they had been taught. They concluded that our formation should consist of obedience, sacrifice, and spirituality. It was their job to alter our persona so we could show our willingness to serve God in any way we were directed—without question. I was often chided for my independent spirit. I didn't mean to be disobedient, but when I saw things to be done, I went ahead and did them without permission. I made many reparations for not following the rules precisely.

Teaching was the focus of our Community. I was privileged to obtain an excellent education that I could have never afforded myself—both a bachelor's and master's degree in education.

However, some of us were still adhering to traits that were unacceptable in our Community. These included noncommitment to blind obedience and nonacceptance of having our personalities stifled.

But then, the times were changing. As the world was changing, I felt compelled to change with it. Pope John XXIII wrote a document asking nuns to "open their convent windows" to see where we were most needed. For me, that meant dedicating myself to serve God's needy people: the homeless; battered women and children; incarcerated women…anywhere I was needed.

However, I couldn't fulfill the pope's directives within the parameters of our Community rules and regulations. I was told that I was a *teacher*, not a social worker.

Through much prayer and personal discernment, I made the decision to answer the pope's call by taking the next step in my journey: separating myself from my religious Community.

Becoming a "rebel" nun left me with unraveled feelings and some guilt for breaking the vows I took to devote my life to God. I was saying goodbye to an ***impossible dream*** so I could pursue one that was ***possible f***or me.

1
Chapter

◞

1947: STARTING MY JOURNEY

As the train pulled into Chicago's Union Station, my five friends and I eagerly ran to board it. We settled in quickly, and then, as the train was pulling away, I glanced out the window and saw my parents waving goodbye. In my enthusiasm to begin my new adventure, I hadn't given a single thought to how they were feeling. My mother was wiping away tears. In my selfishness, I couldn't believe she'd cry when I was feeling so happy. I figured, "She'll get over it." How often I later regretted that thought.

My friends and I settled in for the two hour ride to the motherhouse in Wisconsin where our lives would be changed forever. We talked about the reason each of us decided to enter the religious life. These ranged from infatuation with nuns who taught them, to feeling a Call to make the world a better place.

My reason was simple: I had a great admiration for nuns who practiced humanness as well as spirituality. These nuns were friendly, personable, and generous with their time. They came to our basketball games, and they directed some of our school plays. They encouraged us to participate on the debate team, and they assisted us with difficult assignments. They taught us ways to pray, and they prayed with us. These were the nuns who attracted me to the religious life. I wanted to be just like them.

Before departing for the novitiate, my original plan had been to attend the nursing school where my mother earned her degree. She was delighted that I was following in her footsteps. However, I was impressed when Sister Marie Suzanne, one of the nuns from school, told me she thought I would be a perfect candidate for the novitiate. The more I thought about it, the more enthusiastic I became about this idea. That's when I changed my mind about nursing.

Since the novitiate entrance date was only a month away, there wasn't a lot of time to prepare for it. Even though my mother was disappointed, and she didn't approve of my choice, she provided the money I needed to purchase the required items. She also rushed to sew all the garments I needed.

My only other recollection of that journey is that Dorothy pulled out her cigarettes and offered them to us. We figured this would be our last chance to smoke, so we made the best of it. Although I'd never smoked, I thought I might as well take advantage of this opportunity. Ugh!

We were met at the train station by three smiling nuns who welcomed us, introduced themselves, and then took us to the novitiate where we would spend the next two and a half years preparing spiritually and educationally for our next steps in life. The building was huge and very imposing, but that didn't daunt me. I would not be intimidated by anything deterring me from answering God's Call.

Upon our arrival, the first order of business was to present Sister Dolores, our postulant mistress, with the required two-hundred dollar dowry. This was the money that symbolized my desire to become a Bride of Christ. Since my parents had no other means of fulfilling this obligation, they reluctantly cashed in my life insurance policy so I could pursue my dream of consecrating my life to God.

Later on, Sister Dolores went through our luggage to check our cotton "lingerie" and other items we were required to bring. These included the following:

- six pairs of wide-legged panties that reached to our knees
- six long-sleeved cotton shirts
- six pairs of black cotton stockings
- three black petticoats
- three pinstriped petticoats
- six linen handkerchiefs
- twelve "bird's-eye" napkins (for those monthly episodes of nature)
- two cotton nightgowns

We were also expected to bring a trunk of a specified size, three sets of towels and face cloths, and two pairs of black nurse's shoes. After Sister Dolores completed her inspection of all our belongings, she validated our toiletries by placing an approval tag on each item that was permitted:

- one tube of toothpaste
- one toothbrush
- one container of deodorant
- one small can of talcum powder
- one bar of soap

- one comb
- one hairbrush

All other items were confiscated, and they magically disappeared. Sister Dolores said that when we needed to replenish our toiletries, we could request them from our parents.

2

Chapter

1947: POSTULANT

Dinner was next on our agenda. We ate in the refectory (*dining room*), where we saw novices and the "older" postulants who had started their journey three months previously. They were all smiling and welcoming us to the life they loved so much.

After dinner, we had recreation where we met many more novices and the other eighteen members of our Band who had arrived earlier that day. These were the women with whom I would travel through the novitiate, every step of the way.

Next, we each met our novice assistant. These were novices who were selected to help us find our way during our postulancy. My novice assistant was Sister Mary Jeanine. She said we would spend time together the next day so she could explain some of the rules to me. She would make sure I arrived at designated places on time, and she would be available to answer any of my questions.

Suddenly the bell rang for night prayers. Everyone (except our Band) immediately stopped talking and lowered her eyes for Profound Silence—a time when no one looked at anyone or spoke to anyone until after breakfast the following morning, unless there was an emergency.

While all the other nuns prepared for bed in silence, we were still giggling and laughing nervously. We were discovering what it was like to brush our teeth, take our baths, and get into our nightgowns in *supposed* silence. As we stood in the large bathroom, we whispered to each other and talked about our new life. We even discussed what religious names we were going to choose. Finally, an older nun came into the bathroom to shush us.

We were told the rising bell would ring at five o'clock a.m., and we would have exactly fifteen minutes to get to our chapel places. This persuaded me to get moving to my cubicle It was surrounded by sheets that were hanging on poles to separate each of us from everyone else. It felt strange to know there were many people in the room, while I was a*lone* in this huge dormitory. As time went on, when I wasn't sleeping well, I heard some Sisters snoring, talking in their sleep, or crying.

I climbed into my little cot quickly to get some sleep before our early rising. However, my mind was whirling with all this strange activity. It was the beginning of a whole new life—a life I was thrilled to begin.

Regarding the dormitories, we soon learned that since the building was very old, bats had taken up residence in them. During the night, the bats flew over us, flapping their wings and making strange noises. Sometimes, during the day, we were startled when we found bats sleeping behind pictures or furniture. What a surprise! Although exterminators came regularly, the bats continued their escapades every night. We learned to accept this experience and *offer it up to God* as a sign of our love for Him. One morning when I awoke, a bat was sitting on my knee. Because it was the time of Profound Silence, I didn't scream, but I am amazed I could control myself so well.

That first morning, when the early bell rang, I immediately jumped out of bed. Even though I was bleary-eyed, I managed to get to morning prayers on time. I was happy to see that I shared a prie-dieu (*bench and kneeler*) with my novice assistant, Sister Mary Jeanine. She assisted me in the chapel by showing me the correct page when I lost the place in my prayer book. Later on, she helped me put all my clothes and toiletries in the right places, and she even helped me sew my number, 98, on all my clothing. Throughout the day, I asked her loads of questions, and she patiently answered them all.

During morning prayers, all the nuns chanted the *Office* (*book of psalms*), and we spent some time meditating and attending Mass. Then we all headed for breakfast in the refectory where all the postulants, novices, and professed Sisters were seated.

I was eager to tell my new friends about my experience in the dormitory, and what it was like to sleep on a cot in a little cubicle. To my dismay, all the smiling faces were gone. Everyone was engrossed in the meditative reading being bellowed by a novice. She was obviously selected for this duty because of her reading skills and her ability to project her voice. We soon learned this was the tradition for most meals. Conversation during mealtime was reserved for Sundays, holidays, and special occasions, such as the arrival of new postulants.

The best thing about breakfast was the warm, mouthwatering, sweet rolls; they were freshly baked by one of the Sisters in the on-site bakery. We were encouraged to eat as many as we liked because, as they said, "a good appetite is a sign of a good vocation." These rolls were extremely tempting, so it didn't seem to matter that my skirt was getting tighter by the day.

Meals were served family style—four people for each serving

of food. We were instructed to take some of everything, whether we liked it or not. Since I'd been a picky eater at home, this was not an easy task for me. The worst part was the coffee! I'd always disliked this beverage. (I still do.) I filled my cup three-quarters full of milk before the server reached me; I learned to gulp down the coffee and not make a face while doing so.

After breakfast, we each had a specific employment *(task)* where we were assigned to complete such duties as cleaning floors, keeping a bathroom clean, taking soiled clothes to the laundry, assisting in the kitchen, cleaning the stairs on our knees, washing windows, and many other household chores that kept everything in spic and span order.

When the bell rang, it was time for us to leave our tasks and head for instructions. Since we were new postulants, we went to a separate room for our directives. The first thing we were told was, "The postulancy is a six-month probation period. During this time the superiors will observe all applicants to see if they are worthy to become novices." I was ready and willing to get started immediately. I wanted to be the best and most beloved Bride of Christ He'd ever seen.

Just as other Communities trained their postulants, we were provided with a list of rules that grew longer each day! These included:

- Only speak during recreation periods; otherwise, speak only for charity, politeness, or necessity. (*That meant very little to me at the time.*)
- Don't run on the stairs. (*Whoever walked on stairs?*)
- Do not use mirrors. (*So, how could we comb our hair correctly?*)
- Always keep custody of the eyes. *(eyes lowered).*

- Be sure to sew your number on all personal items as soon as possible.

- Don't have more than six needles in your needle case.

- Never leave any thread in needles.

- Don't have more than three items for mending in your sewing box.

- When placing your clothes in the cupboards, always keep the round edges facing front.

- Never keep any toiletries that don't carry an approved tag.

- Don't swing your arms. (*That was a hard directive to follow.*)

- Never rush. (*another hard rule*)

- Always rise from bed the moment you hear the bell.

- Always stand when a Superior enters the room.

- Always back out of a Superior's office so as not to turn your back on her.

- Any gift you receive should be turned in immediately so it can be shared with others.

- When passing another Sister, look up and greet her by smiling at her guardian angel.

It was hard for us to memorize all the rules, so we had daily reminders. We soon learned that the ordinary penance for small infractions was to kiss the floor. Although I thought this was a silly practice, I thought, "If that's what God wanted me to do, so be it." When the Superior rang the bell, instructions were over.

Our next step was to be tested for the choir. We all wanted to be in this group, not only because we realized what a great privilege it was, but we heard that non-choir Sisters performed housework while the choir was practicing.

Sister Frances Cecile was the music director who decided whether or not we could join this magnificent choir. When testing us, she played a pitch on the piano and asked us to duplicate it. When it was my turn, she played many notes; I made an effort to match each one. I thought I wasn't doing it right because she continued to play other tones for me to match. She finally asked me if I'd ever sung in a group because of my extensive range of musical tones. I never realized how fortunate I was to have this gift of song.

When I told my family I was in the choir, they could hardly believe it because my older sister, Colleen, was always the singer and dancer in our family. My parents said they were proud of me, and they looked forward to visiting me every three months when they would have a chance to hear the novitiate choir, and know that I was part of it.

Next, we were sent to the workroom of Sister Aloysius, the novitiate seamstress. She determined whether or not we could continue wearing brassieres. Those of us who were larger were granted permission to wear a binder that Sister Aloysius provided; our regular bras were impounded. Smaller people were told they didn't need to wear a bra at all. This was hard for me to accept, but again, I was ready and willing to do whatever it took to be a good Sister!

Before lunch, the bell rang for us to assemble in the chapel to review all our indiscretions of the morning. We prayed that we would correct any misdeeds because they displeased our Savior so much.

The issue I "owned" most often was my dislike of Sister Angela. She and I had graduated together from the same high school, and we had been good friends. However, in the novitiate, she became a different person—a "Goody-Two-Shoes,"

When I made my issue known to Sister Dolores, my

penance was to sit next to Sister Angela at least twice during our recreation periods. Sister Angela obviously experienced the same dislike of me, so when we sat together, our time was extremely strained. *(Even Jesus didn't like some people!)*

At another conference, I told Sister Dolores I'd like to be a nurse's aide in the infirmary. Since I had worked in that capacity during my high school years, I thought this would be an appropriate position for me. I was told to **never** think about that again because it was definitely a temptation of the devil. She said I had entered a *teaching* Community, not one in the medical field.

During my following conferences with Sister Dolores, she frequently reviewed this issue with me. She asked if I was disobeying her counsel by continuing to dwell on my desire to assist our ill and older Sisters. When I confessed that I was, she said I should ask God's forgiveness, and pray that I would become willing to do His Will. I did this, but my love of nursing never diminished.

When Sister Dolores and I finished that conference, it was time for lunch. Our food was homemade, and it was usually quite appetizing. Even though we were supposed to take some of everything served, I was often squeamish when I didn't know what I was eating. Once I discovered I'd eaten *brains*. Then I was even more skeptical of unknown foods.

After lunch, all the novices, postulants, and professed Sisters went to the recreation room where we sat in a circle that encompassed the entire room. We were allowed to chat with the person on either side of us after the presiding superior rang the bell. However, we could never discuss anything about our families, how we felt about any of the rules, or what we thought about another Sister.

This was the time when we were expected to mend our

clothes, sew buttons on them, or darn our stockings. Apparently my shoes didn't fit properly, so I often had holes in the heels of my stockings. None of the other postulants had this problem; they'd snicker when they saw that I had stockings to darn again.

When the presiding superior rang the bell, we all proceeded to the chapel to pray the rosary. Class assignments, household chores, conferences, or choir practice filled our afternoons.

During the early afternoons, Sister Mary Jeanine often spent more time with me. I appreciated all she did for me, especially when she gave me a tour of the entire novitiate grounds; that was over and above her assigned duties.

However, after a few days, she realized I was getting a crush on her, so she didn't spend as much time with me. I was disappointed, but I realized I'd pushed her away by my constant efforts to be with her.

During the second week of our novitiate, we began attending classes. I was only a mediocre student, but I loved my courses — particularly children's literature. Other classes included general psychology, philosophy of education, and functional grammar. A great deal of planning time was required for these classes, but our preparation periods were very limited. Organization was a "must."

All courses were conducted in the morning. These were held in various campus buildings, as well as in the novitiate. Since there were only ten minutes between classes, we were obliged to hurry along, and even run on the stairs to avoid being late for our next class. This was unacceptable behavior, so I frequently accused myself of this "rushing" misdemeanor, and I usually received the same penance: kiss the floor. (I wondered how we were expected to walk sedately and still get to our classes on time.)

Each day was a new experience. Little did I know that

learning rules, taking a few classes, and eating silent meals were not all that lay in store for me. During the entire month of August, our recreations were spent chatting and laughing with each other while we picked strawberries in the blazing noon sun and blackberries or blueberries in the waning hours of daylight. We were allowed to eat a few berries, but if we judged we'd eaten too many, we requested a penance — which was readily supplied.

Those long-sleeved cotton undershirts, black cotton stockings, and woolen uniforms stuck tightly to us, especially during these high-noon outings! The "faint of heart" were given special permission to take an afternoon bath, but the "strong hearted" (like me) bore the sacrifice of a simple sponge bath until they were scheduled for a real one --- usually three times each week.

We had some special recreation periods, especially on Friday afternoons. When the weather was pleasant, we enjoyed a walk to the lake. Sister Dolores allowed us to share candy that had been gifts to other postulants. In spring and summer we played volley ball and tennis. Once we had a Ping-pong tournament. (I won.) In the fall, we collected colorful leaves, and in the winter we collected fir branches and berries so we could decorate the refectory and the community room. When it snowed, we enjoyed making snowballs and building snowmen. We even had some snowball fights. If we encountered inclement weather, we stayed inside and worked with crafts. I enjoyed this activity because it gave me an opportunity to be creative without a requirement to produce a project under specific instructions.

We were ecstatic when both our novices' and professed Sisters' choirs were invited to sing at a fundraising concert at the Metropolitan City Center. Each day, Sister Frances Cecile held special choir practices in preparation for this concert. It was a magnificent program. We sang renditions of Irish and Scottish music, some patriotic songs, and some old favorites, along with more serious devotional numbers. To perform on this hallowed stage, to a capacity audience, was an incredible experience.

A recording was made of this performance. Not only our families and friends purchased the records, but when they were distributed to music stores, they were quickly "snatched up" by music lovers and those who wanted to enjoy a nuns' chorus. My parents purchased a record for me; I still have it.

During the holidays, the superiors entered into the spirit of the season. Extra recreation periods and festivities were prepared for us.

Christmas was amazing. Postulants and novices decorated the chapel and recreation room with berries and branches from our own bushes and fir trees. Before the midnight Mass, our novitiate choir sang traditional Christmas carols, and our music during the Mass was incredible. Everyone said we sounded like angels singing from heaven.

Poinsettias and more than fifty candles decorated the altar. It was surprising to see how quickly Sister Rose Marie lit so many candles. After this was accomplished, Father George walked up and down the aisles blessing everyone with holy water and carrying burning incense, a symbol of the faithful's prayers rising to heaven. An empty crib had been set up, and the youngest postulant carried the Baby Jesus figurine and placed it in the crib. Joy reigned in everyone's heart!

After Mass we went to the refectory for some oyster stew. Although I didn't care for it, this was a delicacy that most Sisters enjoyed. I managed to skim the milk off the top of the bowl to avoid taking any oysters.

Christmas Day was also impressive. Our novitiate choir sang at Mass, and once again, we were told our music was a real gift to everyone. In the afternoon we went for a brisk walk and enjoyed the wonders of the day – nature at its finest — snow-covered trees, magnificent clouds, birds that hadn't flown north, squirrels racing with one another – we even saw a deer. When we returned, to the novitiate, our cheeks were rosy and we felt exhilarated. We sang Christmas carols and enjoyed hot chocolate. Peace and joy reigned everywhere.

However, there was one unhappy event that occurred during the holidays. All postulants were told that Sister Amelia, who was our novice mistress, wished to speak with us in her office— one-by-one. As we stood in line and watched each postulant emerge from Sister Amelia's office, we became more curious as to what was happening in there.

When it was my turn to enter, both the postulant and novice mistress stood there and addressed me very sternly. I was told to lift my skirt and show them the number on my stockings. They exchanged glances with each other and seemed surprised when they saw my number – 98.

Although I had no concept of what had just taken place, I knew it was something serious. I was directed to return to my study period and speak with no one regarding this experience.

We eventually discovered that some postulants were missing stockings from their cabinets. Since I was always mending mine, the superiors figured I was probably the culprit. When I was told later that I was the suspect, I was humiliated and indignant. How could anyone even imagine I would do such a thing?

I made reparation for thinking ill of my Superiors and for showing my feelings. I was definitely offended! However, we were being taught not to feel too happy, sad, angry, tired, or lonely. These were faults that were considered intolerable for one who was seeking perfection.

It seemed there were always more rules to learn. Besides

those we were taught during our regular instruction periods, there were other violations that included:

- Innocently telling another postulant that a member of our Band left the novitiate and returned home. I knew this because her bed in the dormitory was stripped, and there was nothing in her cubicle to indicate she was still there. I soon learned this was a matter *never* to be discussed.

- Not observing the rules to kneel when sweeping the stairs even though I was stooping because I fell and hurt my knee.

- Showing off my talent of being a high-speed typist. I was told to slow down because it appeared I was boasting about my typing abilities.

- Comforting a postulant when she was crying. This was not acceptable because she should have gone to one of the Superiors, not to me.

- Going upstairs without permission to change my pad during my monthly episodes of nature, even when there was no superior around to provide the necessary approval.

I had a hard time accepting these violations. They didn't make sense to me. However, I thought if I wanted to be a good postulant, I needed to follow all the rules, not just the ones I could accept readily.

Meanwhile, I was secretly pleased that I was learning to conform to the rules and regulations, as well as to the counsel I received from my superiors I just knew, that in the eyes of God, I was progressing well, even though I never received any indication of this from my Superiors.

After three months, we received our religious names by

which we would be known forever. This formality took place in Reverend Mother's office after Sister Dolores alleged we had all met the requirements for this ceremony.

Before this special day, we submitted three choices of our preferred names to Sister Dolores—with no assurance that any of them would be selected for us. In that case, Reverend Mother would choose a name she thought was appropriate. None of our choices could be the same as any living Sister's, and a three year waiting period was prescribed before the name of a deceased Sister could be granted to anyone,

I have always had a special devotion to our Blessed Mother, so one of the names I submitted was *Sister Mary*. I didn't dream I'd actually receive it because I didn't feel worthy of such an honor. Reverend Mother went down the line presenting new names and engraved Community pendants to each postulant. My heart was pounding as I waited for my name to be called. When Mother said, "You will be known as Sister Mary," I couldn't believe my ears! Many Sisters had requested this name previously, so I felt especially honored to receive it.

After this ceremony, we went to the chapel for noon prayers. Our novice friends who were already there were waiting for the news of our changed names. As we walked down the church aisle, we *disobediently* showed them our fingers, indicating which choice we'd received.

We had recreation at lunch time, and each postulant stood up to tell everyone her new name. This was a joyous occasion, except for Sister Ann who was given one of the *selected names* chosen by Reverend Mother. She cried all through lunch because she hated the name she'd have forever. After lunch Reverend Mother called her aside and said she could change her name, but in her humility Sister Ann opted to keep it.

I was thrilled with my new name! I wrote to my parents

to inform them about it; I knew they would rejoice with me. However, because I expressed so much enthusiasm, this entailed making reparation for showing my feelings. All these feelings—good or bad—were to be eliminated from our persona so we could always stay humble in the presence of God. I was becoming a robot.

After we received our new names and pendants, we were expected to strive more steadily for excellence in our pursuit of perfection. It was difficult to break my persona, but I was willing to let them try because I thought Jesus would love me more if I did everything just as I was told. Now that I had the precious name of Sister Mary, I prayed to our Blessed Mother to help me follow all the rules presented to me.

However, it wasn't long before I reverted to some of my old ways. For instance, when I passed other Sisters in the hall, I did look at them and greet their guardian angels, but I still used this opportunity to study the magnificent architecture and mosaics of our huge building; then I looked out the windows at God's nature.

There were other infractions of the rules, too. We had no TV or radio, so I ordinarily didn't know what was going on in the world. I was always delighted when one of the Sisters cleaned the bathroom floors and placed newspapers on them to help dry the tiles. Of course I took this opportunity to read the papers and catch up on the news, even though it wasn't the news of the day.

Rushing and swinging my arms were other infractions of the rules, but somehow my arms just kept swinging, and I kept rushing. However, I wasn't the only one who swung her arms. Our whole Band was sent to the college gymnasium where the PE teacher instructed us to walk around the building without moving our arms. (The whole time we were there, the instructor shook her head in disbelief that she had received such an assignment.)

When I was cleaning windows, I tried not to view my reflection to see how I looked, but I didn't succeed very well.

All these infractions were observed and recorded by our superiors; they were continually reviewing our actions to assure themselves that after our six-month probation as postulants, we were prepared to become novices. I began to feel confused because I was so frequently chided for doing something wrong when I thought I was doing it right. I started believing that I couldn't do anything in the approved manner, and my superiors didn't deflect these thoughts.

Humility and Blind Obedience were the mantra for each day! Humility was no problem for me! I was constantly being humbled, so I tried to grasp the idea that my superiors' efforts to humiliate me should make me humble. Not so!

Blind obedience was another story. I tried desperately to embrace this directive, which was doing what a superior requested—without question. However, I often thought this was peculiar because many times I knew I could do something better than the way I was told to do it. I tried not to show my feelings, but I usually wasn't successful because my face showed my annoyance. This did not go unnoticed by my superiors, so the usual reparation was required: kiss the floor. Even though I wasn't getting much recognition from my superiors, I just knew God was pleased with my effort. Of course I never told anyone how I felt because I would be accused of having pride.

Once each month we enjoyed receiving mail from our parents. We were allowed to send them letters at that time, but we could no longer have any correspondence with our friends— not even to acknowledge their letters or cards. This was to help us detach from friends, and eventually, from our families. Sadly, our friends thought we had forgotten about them.

All incoming and outgoing mail was read first by one of our superiors. If we wrote something negative about our lifestyle, we were told to rewrite the letter in a more positive manner. If any letter we received had bad news in it, we were called into Sister Dolores's office where she told us about this matter before we read it. When my grandfather died, I appreciated the kind way that Sister Dolores told me about it.

During the course of this year, I received a letter from Jeanette, my younger sister, who was married to Peter. She said she was considering divorcing him. Then *he* wrote to tell me how much he loved her, asking me to plead with her not to divorce him. I was admonished not to answer either of these letters because I was supposed to be detaching myself from all family matters. Consequently, my sister and her husband thought I didn't care about their issue. I never heard from either of them again regarding this matter. In fact, I didn't hear from Jeanette for more than seven years.

Was my postulancy easy? No! It seemed the harder I tried to do things right, the more they got twisted. There were just too many rules to apply at all times. I didn't always keep custody of the eyes, I didn't stop running on the stairs when I was late for class or an assembly, and I was still frequently late for morning prayers because I couldn't move fast enough to get to the chapel in the allotted time. I made all my reparations, but I had a hard time conforming to all these rules.

I negatively impressed the superiors who were grading us and checking on everything we did. I was often called into one of their offices to be admonished for taking things upon myself instead of obtaining permission to do them. At the time, it always seemed to me that I was doing the right thing. I had reasons for what I did, but I usually wasn't allowed to express them—even when I knew I was correct in my thinking. When my superiors directed me to do projects *their* way, I tried to help them understand there was a better way to do what they were requesting. My advice was never accepted, and I was told I needed to respect authority by doing what I was told to do—the way I was told to do it. As always, I had a problem trying to hide my feelings. That didn't go unnoticed, so once again I was making reparation for something I didn't think was deserved.

3

Chapter

1948: TRANSITION DAY

It was a joyous and exciting time as we prepared to begin our
next step in the novitiate. We made an eight-day retreat that
was a time of prayer, personal discernment, spiritual reading,
lectures on God's love for us, and reflections on the lives of
major saints. It was a time of Profound Silence. During this
retreat, the superiors decided whether or not each of us was
eligible to become a novice.

Those who successfully completed our six-month probation
period were privileged to take part in our long-awaited Transition
Day ceremony. We donned lovely wedding gowns and veils,
indicating we were truly Brides of Christ. We were even allowed
to wear a touch of makeup that day. (If our families couldn't
afford to purchase a wedding gown for us, one that had been
worn previously was altered accordingly. I wore a gorgeous dress
that was modified specifically for me. I loved its simplicity.)

When we were all dressed and ready, we stopped in a large
parlor for a ten-minute visit with our parents so they could see
us in our wedding gowns. My parents were delighted to see me

in my lovely dress, but they were sorry no one was allowed to take any pictures.

Since four of our Band members were no longer with us, twenty postulants proceeded to the big church in preparation for our long procession to the main altar. It must have been an incredible sight to see all of us betrothed women process to the altar to receive our Holy Habits. After the bishop prayed with us, we left the altar, carrying our treasured Habits to the rear of the church. We were met by Sisters who brought us to a special room where they were assigned to cut our hair and help us dress in our new attire: woolen skirts and capes, starched collars and caps, and our white veils.

Meanwhile, the Sisters who were professing their vows processed to the altar in groups to make their solemn promises to God. Our novices who had spent two and a half years preparing for this day took their first vows. After their white veils were exchanged for black ones, they received their long rosaries, which were worn from their waist to their knee. Then a group of professed Sisters renewed their vows for one year, and others took them for three years. The last group professed their final vows *forever.*

Then we, the new novices, processed back to the altar in our new attire. We recited prayers where we promised God we would make every effort to become the Sisters He desired us to be. Despite the fact that I had many challenges during my postulancy, I loved the religious life and my Sisters. Receiving my Habit was one of the greatest joys I had ever known.

Lunch was extremely festive. The incoming postulants were admiring our new novices' garb, and we were trying to adapt to our novel attire. The newly professed Sisters were eagerly discussing their upcoming missions (*designated assignments*). They could hardly wait to take their next step—meeting their companion Sisters, and preparing their lessons for the grade level they were assigned to teach.

My parents came to see me receive my Holy Habit, but they were only allowed to stay for that one day. They could visit me every three months, and they never missed this opportunity. I took it for granted they would be there! I never realized how inconvenient and expensive travel was for them. My mother usually came alone because my dad often worked on weekends.

Mom took a cab to the train station in Chicago and a train from Chicago to Wisconsin where she stayed at a small motel in town. After she registered at the motel, she took a cab to the novitiate. Only then was she able to visit with me.

Mom usually arrived around eleven o'clock a.m. After forty-five minutes I reluctantly left her for prayers and lunch while she waited in the parlor. After lunch, I could spend my one-hour recreation period with her, but then I had to leave her to return to the chapel to pray the rosary. She left by four o'clock because that's when we chanted the *Office*. Although we had so little time together, Mom always thought it was worth her trip to see me.

As I was learning to become more spiritual, I was also learning to become more detached from my family—and more selfish! At no time was any food or drink offered to my mother, and I never thought about any of her needs. As I look back now, I am appalled at my lack of sensitivity.

One Thanksgiving Day, it was snowing heavily. My mother's train was delayed, so she didn't arrive until almost two o'clock, just in time for me to leave for prayers. When I came to the parlor later, she asked me about our Thanksgiving dinner. I gave her all the details without even stopping to realize she'd had nothing to eat while she waited for me.

At four o'clock she left for her motel. However, because of

the inclement weather, her cab was delayed. When it didn't arrive on time, Mom thought some of the nuns might not like her standing near the door, so she started walking in the deep, blinding snow. I was getting more detached from my family, so I never even thought about her trekking in the storm.

The day after Thanksgiving, I visited with Mom at the usual times—a total of about three and a half hours. She always told me she was proud of me, but when she left that day, she seemed sad. I never considered her feelings, so I didn't attempt to understand why she felt that way.

When I think back and realize how much effort she made to see me for a few hours, I am so sorry I took her for granted. She never missed an opportunity to visit me. She never complained that no one—myself included—brought her something to drink. She never complained about being tired after her trip. She never discussed the cost of her trip. She sacrificed far more than I did, and I didn't even know it. I was quickly becoming conditioned to believe our customs and rules overruled any of my mother's needs.

4

Chapter

1948: FIRST-YEAR NOVICE

We were now first-year novices, preparing for the day we would take our vows. There were special instructions for novices. These included: not becoming too friendly with other Sisters; not holding hands with each other; and not touching anyone unnecessarily. Ideally, we were supposed to love each Sister equally and show no preferences. When possible, we were also encouraged to recreate in groups of three or more. Obviously, this was related to avoiding lesbianism, a new concept for me.

Even children from our families were never to be held —this included babies. One novice left the novitiate because she was not allowed to hold her new baby brother. This rule was later carried over to our classrooms where we were admonished not to hug or touch little children. However, when the children ran up to me looking for a hug, I never pushed them away. When I had playground duty, I usually played games with the little children where we held hands. Although I was reprimanded for this many times, it was one rule to which I never totally conformed.

Later that month, we transferred from our chapel to the

big church; it was a lot farther from our dormitory. Now it was even more difficult for me to move quickly enough to brush my teeth, get dressed with all my novel new clothes, and travel to the big church within the fifteen minutes allotted. I could never figure out how some Sisters were ready in the short time allowed; some were even waiting at the top of the stairs to leave for the church when the bell rang. I can't help but think they got up early, which was against the rules.

I'm sorry to say I was late for morning prayers on many occasions, and my superior told me that Jesus was not pleased with me. She said I was making His suffering on the cross even more excruciating. That was the last thing I wanted to do to the God I loved so much.

This year, half our day was spent in prayer and meditation. The other half was designated for manual tasks that included: scrubbing long halls on our hands and knees; making beds for clergy who frequently made retreats at our motherhouse; washing and ironing veils, drapes and tablecloths; scouring huge pots and pans in the scullery (*kitchen*); sorting clothes in the hot laundry; assisting in the sewing room; washing windows; polishing all wooden door frames, and more.

My first assignment was to iron white veils for novices so they would all have a fresh one at the beginning of each week. We had two hours each morning to complete this task, but I knew we'd never finish on time because my partner, Sister Ingrid, prayed her rosary between each veil she ironed. I was aggravated, but I couldn't say anything because that wouldn't be charitable, and I would be showing my feelings of frustration. However, when Sister Amelia realized the veils weren't going to be ready on time, I received special permission to spend some afternoon hours ironing them by myself.

Another of my assignments was to scrub a bedroom floor

in one of the college dormitories. I was emptying a bucket of dirty water and filling it with clean water when Sister Brigid Marie, the maintenance supervisor, shrieked, "You don't need to change the water! It doesn't matter if it's dirty — just so the rags are clean!" This mistake required me to make reparation for wasting soapy water. However, I still tried to be joyful, because I just knew God was smiling on my efforts.

If we needed a slight respite, we were allowed to go to the refectory for a little collation (*snack*). The rolls left over from breakfast were on a tray, and we could help ourselves to this treat. We ate in silence, and then we returned to our task at hand.

My next assignment was to assist our cook, Sister Emily Marie, in the kitchen. She prepared meals for more than 250 Sisters—novices, postulants, and professed Sisters. I felt sorry for her because many times the novices who were assigned to help her were more hindrance than help.

Sister Emily Marie could not attend prayers with the other Sisters because of her cooking schedule, so she had a different prayer arrangement to accommodate her needs. When Sister Mary Celine and I were assigned to help in the kitchen, Sister Emily Marie left tasks for us to complete while she was gone. Being left to ourselves, we made some bad decisions. I threw away a large canister of skim milk that looked like it was spoiled. Unfortunately, Sister Emily Marie always used that for baking, so I was in big trouble.

Sister Mary Celine was told to separate the eggs—hundreds of them. She put all the brown ones in one container and the white ones in another. Poor Sister Emily Marie! Of course, she was very unhappy with us. She said that the kind of assistance we provided made her hesitant to leave the kitchen, even for her prayers.

When our novice mistress heard about our calamities in the kitchen, she said our next assignment would be in the scullery, where we would wash the pots and pans used for meal preparations. These were so huge we could almost fit inside them.

We were expected to make our own Habit, but I never mastered that task. I couldn't sew my circular cape no matter how hard I tried. I was discouraged when Sister John, the home economics teacher, required me to rip out my sewing over and over. One 0f the novices had pity on me. Without checking with Sister John, she exchanged my cape for her apron so I could sew on a straight line while she handled the more complex task of sewing on the curve.

Our employments and refectory seating were changed every week. Some novices were given the "privilege" of sitting at the same table as Sister Amelia. She had diabetes, so special food was prepared for her. Despite the fact that we were supposed to eat some of everything, she usually didn't eat her prepared food; she passed it down the table to us. We had our own meal, but she expected us to finish hers, too. As can be imagined, none of us was thrilled when we were assigned to her table.

I was delighted to be selected as a reader in the refectory. I prepared the readings diligently. After each meal I was informed about any words I had mispronounced. Despite my preparation, I still had some mishaps:

- I mispronounced the word *heifer*. I said "hee-fer." Many Sisters grew up on farms, so I could actually hear their intake of breath as I was reading.

- On one occasion I prepared the daily meditation for the wrong day. One of the Sisters left her table to notify me of my mistake. I was not prepared for this setback, but I attempted to read the correct meditation. Unfortunately, I mispronounced words like agnosticism and asceticism.

This was a hard year because I felt exhausted most of the time. Taking a nap was out of the question, and complaining was only a cause for reparation; I learned to tolerate my fatigue. As a consequence, I often fell asleep during meditation and spiritual reading periods.

Meanwhile, I started wondering if I was being brainwashed. Since I was continually reprimanded for breaking the rules, I started wondering if I was I really doing everything because that's what *God* expected of me? Was I doing *God's Will* ... or that of my superiors? I was beginning to think like a rebel nun.

I had many conferences with my superiors who repeatedly chastised me for various infractions of the rules—especially for not becoming a more spiritual person because I often slept in chapel during meditation periods. (It seemed that whenever I sat down, I immediately fell asleep.) Even though I was trying to conform to all the rules, there were still too many for me to follow. My efforts to do my best never seemed to be enough to please my superiors. Through it all, I never lost my trust in God. I just kept trying to be the person He expected me to be.

A special privilege first-year novices received was to spend all night praying in the Holy Trinity Chapel; an elegant monstrance containing a large Host was exposed on a special altar for veneration—twenty-four hours a day. Although I appreciated being selected for this assignment, I fell asleep in the chapel, instead of praying. I asked God to forgive me, just, as Jesus forgave His apostles when they slept while He was suffering in the Garden of Olives. Of course, I was reprimanded for this weakness. I was told that I'd been given an opportunity to worship the God Who loves me, but Instead of reciprocating His love, I spent my time sleeping.

I finally discovered how our superiors knew so many things we did wrong, even when they weren't around to see us. Individual novices were given the task of observing us and keeping a record of all our infractions of the rules. These included the following:

- not keeping the hem of our Habits clean
- having the incorrect number of needles in our sewing box
- having more than three items for mending in our sewing box
- not folding items in our cabinets with the round edges out
- not greeting a Sister's guardian angel
- running on the stairs
- talking or laughing outside of recreation periods
- not keeping custody of the eyes
- swinging our arms
- recreating with the same person more than three times in one month
- not taking some of each dish of food that was served
- sleeping in the chapel
- having toiletry items without the appropriate tags
- talking about our family
- having spots on our capes or large collars

One Sunday each month, the novices who recorded our failings read their lists of those who had not followed the rules precisely. When a Sister was accused of an infraction, she stood until all charges were completed for that issue. Some novices snickered when they heard such pronouncements as "Sister

Mary—running on the stairs five times." I was usually on many lists.

After all the allegations were finished, we knelt before the novice mistress, one-by-one, to ask pardon for not obeying the rules more assiduously. We promised we'd try to do better during the coming month. (By the way, the novices who recorded our misdemeanors were changed every month, so we were unaware of who would have those "plum jobs" the next time. I was never selected.)

The only classes we were allowed to attend as first-year novices were philosophy, Church history, and Bible studies. The most boring ones were Church history and philosophy. These were taught by Father George, a respected priest who had taught novices and postulants for the past forty years. He never gave any assignments or exams, so many of us spent this class preparing letters for our families or completing Bible study assignments. He didn't seem to notice (or care).

Our superiors were aware of the situation, but they didn't try to control it because of their respect for Father George. However, sometimes when we were given a penance to perform, we were told to pay attention during Father George's classes. Of course we were expected to show our notes to Sister Amelia.

5
Chapter

1949: SECOND- YEAR NOVICE

When we became second-year novices, our Band had dwindled to sixteen. Besides our regular schedule of prayer and spirituality, the major part of this year was dedicated to our classes. Our families provided notebooks, typing paper, pens, pencils, and other needed school supplies.

We were deluged with assignments! One course I particularly enjoyed was a speech class taught by a drama teacher. She tested our speaking voices and placed us in groups according to our voice pitches: low, medium, and high. She had us do readings that included sections for individual groups, and other parts for the entire ensemble. The blending of the group's voices was incredible. This class was so unique! I loved every minute of it.

During this year, I was just as fatigued mentally as I had been physically, when I was a first-year novice. However, I loved my classes and looked forward to the day I could teach in my own schoolroom. (When we actually started teaching, we had only one and a half years of classroom preparation—six months as a postulant and one year as a second-year novice.)

One of my major challenges was getting from one college building to another in the fifteen minutes allotted between classes. I was usually rushing so I wouldn't be late for the next class, and of course, this was noted by a novice who was preparing her list of infractions.

All written papers required for our classes were first presented to Sister Amelia; she corrected any errors in syntax, spelling, or grammar. If she found an error in anyone's assignment, that novice was reminded that she needed to address her writing skills. Sister Amelia asked how we could expect to teach young children the proper way of writing if we were lacking in our own skills. This was one platform where I knew I could excel. I was actually *complimented* for my expertise in this area.

As second-year novices, we were allowed to take a bus to observe elementary school classes in town. After observing Mrs. Doherty as she encouraged and assisted her fifth- grade class, we were allowed to take turns teaching some of them. That's when Mrs. Doherty and the other novices critiqued us. Although none of us had any teaching experience, we convinced ourselves that we were qualified to evaluate others.

When it was my turn to teach, I was advised I would be instructing math to seven fifth-graders. I spent a week making charts and organizing papers for my debut. Little did I realize how impractical it was to spend so much time on the preparation for one lesson. Sadly, this was the only practice teaching I had before being sent out on my mission.

My evaluations from Mrs. Doherty and the other novices were excellent. However, Sister Amelia let us know that we all had a long way to go before we could claim any critiquing expertise. The only critiques that bore any weight were those from Mrs. Doherty.

Due to our classes and educational activities, our year as

second-year novices flew by. However, this was one of our last chances to strive for perfection in the novitiate, so our reparations were augmented to more difficult ones. Some of these occurred in the refectory. During dinner, we sat at the table and passed the food to others while we abstained. Another reparation was to absent ourselves from the dinner meal while we stayed in the chapel and prayed. These fasts were not too difficult because our lunch was always stable and satisfying.

I made the mistake of telling Sister Amelia these penances were meaningless to me. She said. "If you can't accept them in the spirit in which they were given, I will find more difficult ones for you." Once again, I realized it was much better to keep my thoughts to myself.

Each week, novices were assigned to serve meals to the other Sisters. Some novices were privileged to serve Reverend Mother's table. I think it was by accident I was assigned to serve her table *once*. I was surprised when I received this employment because only special novices usually had this privilege. I was carrying a tray of oranges, and they fell on the floor *under Reverend Mother's table*. There I was, crawling around on my hands and knees, trying to recover the lost fruit...and then serve it as if nothing happened. I think Reverend Mother was probably laughing, but it wasn't treated as a laughing matter by Sister Amelia. I was never again assigned to serve Reverend Mother's table.

My favorite table was the one where our elderly Sisters needed extra attention. Some of them had odd ways of eating; some even kept talking while the reading was in progress. One Sister drew a line on the tablecloth so she could make sure her dishes were right in front of her and no one else could touch them. Another Sister collected apples and oranges in her apron before the meal began. The kitchen staff merely replaced fruit to the right tables.

No one paid too much attention to these infractions, because each Sister was always treated with dignity and respect. I considered it an honor to serve our Sisters who had physical and mental disabilities. It was easy to reflect that many of them had been heroic in their classrooms, and they had probably been extremely influential with their students. Now it was time to show them my love and appreciation.

6
Chapter

1950: PROFESSION OF FIRST VOWS

By the following year, when we were ready to take our first vows, our Band had dwindled to fourteen. We always looked forward to the yearly Transition Day ceremony where postulants received their Habits, and professed Sisters renewed their vows. When we were called forth, our Band processed to the altar and signed a book that indicated our willingness to dedicate our lives to God.

We knelt as the bishop solemnly prayed over us. Then he asked each of us if we were ready to dedicate our lives to our Savior and accept the responsibilities of our vows. When we each answered in the affirmative, our white veils were exchanged for black ones, and we were presented with our long rosaries. These formalities indicated that we were now professed Sisters who would immediately undertake our teaching careers.

Since it was January, the schools were already in session. We knew we would be assigned either to an overcrowded school that needed an extra teacher, or to a school where we would replace a professed Sister who was returning to the motherhouse to prepare for her final vows.

7

Chapter

❧

MISSIONS: 1950-1951

I was transferred many times throughout the years. Although I never received a direct answer as to why I was transferred, so often, I presumed it may have been because I became too involved with parish activities. Perhaps I was too independent. Perhaps I didn't please my superior. Most times I had no idea why I was transferred, and I wasn't allowed to question the decision.

1950: St. Sebastian School, Wisconsin

When I arrived at this mission, I was surprised to see our living arrangements. This was a house, not a convent. It had only a few bedrooms, so three of us were assigned to one bedroom. I'd never lived in a situation like this, but I soon adapted to it. The hardest part was scheduling our time in the bathroom so we could all get to our prayers on time.

I used to get carsick every morning. This annoyed my superior, Sister Mary Eileen. She told me I'd better get over it, because it seemed I was just looking for attention, and this was not appropriate for a young Sister. Rather than complain again, I pretended I was all right. I suppressed my nausea as best I could.

This school was extremely overcrowded, so I was given part of a second-grade class to teach. The nun who shared these children with me gave me her more advanced students so she could spend more time with those who needed extra help. Little did I realize that she had been so generous! I just presumed all children behaved as well as these did.

It was a pleasure to be in this well-disciplined classroom where the children were very bright. When I wrote the word *eskimo* on the board, one little girl stood up and said, "That word always starts with a capital letter." I began debating with her, but she never backed down. (Of course, she was right!)

Because I'd had so little practice teaching, I had no idea how to handle this large second- grade class. There were teachers' manuals in the classroom, but since we hadn't used them for practice teaching, I didn't know how to utilize them. I didn't realize I was doing anything wrong, so I didn't seek help.

Sister Mary Rita, the supervisor of schools, visited our school and toured every classroom. After she observed my room for a little while, she left without speaking to me. After school, Sister Mary Rita gave every Sister a critique of her teaching methods. When I met with her, she said, "I have never seen a more terrible performance in all my life!" She asked me about teachers' manuals, and I confessed I didn't know how to use them. She was appalled! She assigned one of the nuns to be my mentor so I could develop some acceptable teaching skills.

After being told I was a terrible teacher, I determined I could either "give up," or become one of the finest teachers possible. I chose the latter. I worked hard: I learned to use manuals; study various types of curricula; read every educational magazine I could get my hands on; observe other teachers' classes; and take courses in classroom management at local colleges. It took time, but my efforts finally paid off. I became an outstanding primary teacher, and I taught children to love and appreciate their education.

When I was transferred from this school, I didn't think too much about it. Since I was new, I thought it would be nice to meet some other Sisters.

1951: St. Aloysius Academy, Michigan

I was assigned to a first-grade class that I loved. However, Sister Mary Ida, a second-grade teacher, became ill and was no longer able to teach. Her children were divided between the other second-grade teacher and me. That meant I would now be teaching both first and second grades.

Although it would have been easier to transfer the second-grade children to my classroom, Sister Henrietta, the principal and superior, decided I would relocate my first-grade class to the other room. This meant all my books, bookshelves, charts, teacher's plans, art supplies, and other classroom equipment needed to be transferred from my classroom to the second-grade room.

After school, I was dragging boxes that contained all the essential items I would need in my new classroom. Some eighth-grade boys saw me struggling with the boxes, so they offered to help me. I was grateful for their assistance. However, when they completed the task, they stayed in my classroom and started playing games and drawing on the blackboard. I thanked them and asked them to leave, but they continued to enjoy themselves by playing more blackboard games.

Lo and behold! Sister Mary Charles, an older nun from the fourth-grade classroom across the hall, stepped into my room and declared loudly that the boys didn't belong there. She said emphatically, "You know young nuns aren't supposed to have boys in their classrooms!"

The boys left, but they thought Sister Mary Charles's comments were funny. They were laughing and throwing a ball to each other as they departed. Naturally, my offense was quickly related to Sister Henrietta who told me she was taking special note of this infraction. That usually meant the matter would be reported to Reverend Mother immediately.

Unfortunately, the boys returned the next day. They didn't realize this was so serious for me. Again, Sister Mary Charles saw the boys and reported me a second time.

On Valentine's Day, I was horrified to find that two boys left the school without permission to purchase a box of candy for me. I told them I couldn't accept it, but they left it on my desk. I advised them to get back to their own classroom as quickly as possible, so their long absence wouldn't be noted by their teacher, Sister Henrietta.

Sister Mary Charles was incapable of teaching music to her class, so I was assigned to teach it for her. While I was teaching music in her classroom, she was supposed to teach spelling in mine; however, I discovered she didn't teach anything at all during that period. When I asked the children why their spelling workbooks weren't completed, they said that Sister Mary Charles didn't help them; she just read her newspaper. I couldn't criticize an older Sister, so I was forced to squeeze spelling into my already crowded curriculum, without any question of right or wrong.

When the second-grade class was originally split, most of the children I "inherited" were cooperative and helpful. However, included in this class was a set of twins, John and Jonathon, who were very hyperactive. These boys melted their crayons on the radiator. One of them climbed inside a large wastebasket while the other one rolled it around the room. They put a stuffed animal in the toilet. They opened the windows to let rain come into the room. They sat in other children's seats. They took school supplies from one child's desk and put them in another desk. They were bullies on the playground. They learned to vomit *on request* and they showed this talent frequently.

Because of these boys, it was extremely difficult for the other children to concentrate on their lessons. They eventually learned to ignore the twins so they could progress with their own assignments.

I spoke to the boys' parents, but they shrugged their shoulders and claimed they were unable to control the boys. These parents alleged it was the *school's* responsibility to do its duty by teaching the twins how to act properly. As expected, these uncooperative parents were noncompliant with school rules, and they never helped their boys with homework or other projects.

The highlight of that year was when my dad came to visit me. This time, my mom was unable to come with him. Unfortunately, the visit didn't turn out to be all that we hoped.

Dad was welcomed by the Sisters, but since the rules stated that I couldn't be alone with a man (not even my dad), another Sister was required to sit in the parlor with us. Although she was very pleasant, and she joined in our conversations, Dad had no idea why she was there. When I explained the rules to him, he was horrified and hurt beyond belief. When he left to return home, he hardly said goodbye to anyone, including me. Of course, he never again visited me alone.

When I was transferred from this school, I figured it was probably because I'd been reported twice for having boys in my room, and Reverend Mother had been notified. (I figured correctly!)

8

Chapter

MOTHERHOUSE: WISCONSIN

That summer of 1951, I returned to the motherhouse to take more classes. Besides our classes, one of the highlights of that summer was permission for the Sisters to swim in the college pool. Ordinarily, that pool was drained for the summer, so this was a great surprise. It wasn't announced for a few weeks because some Sisters were secretly assigned to make bathing suits for us. These were seersucker dresses and panties, but no one cared. We just wanted to get in the pool.

The bathing suits were colored according to size. However, the first time they were washed, all the color bleached out, so when we went to the pool, we took any size available.

Coupons for the pool were awarded to everyone. These indicated the time and date the coupons could be used. It was so much fun to see the Sisters negotiating with one another to exchange their coupons for a more preferable time. It was even more fun to see how happy they were when they were in the pool. Sisters who didn't want their coupons gave them to other Sisters so they could have extra hours in the pool.

Besides swimming, when I had time, I enjoyed taking leisurely walks around our campus. One Sunday when I was walking, a young couple asked me if someone might be available to show them around our grounds. Since I was just relaxing, I told them I'd be happy to accompany them on a tour. We visited the grottos, the chapels and various campus buildings. We even inspected the areas near the novitiate. This couple was delightful. They said they were non-Catholic, but they'd heard about our lovely grounds and hoped to have a chance to see them. They weren't disappointed.

They took lots of pictures and continued to insist that I pose in one of them. I rejected this idea over and over because no Sister was supposed to have her picture taken until after she professed her final vows. (I had professed my vows for only one year.) However, the couple was quite persistent about photographing me. Since they weren't Catholic, I didn't think it was appropriate to explain our rules to them. I figured they probably wouldn't understand such a regulation.

After much persuasion, I finally allowed them to take one picture. They were delighted, and I assumed that, under the circumstances, I had done the right thing. Unfortunately, these lovely people sent me a copy of the picture. Since all our mail was opened by a superior, the picture was right there on her desk. I was told I'd been very disobedient, and I was sent to the chapel to ask God's forgiveness for this act of defiance.

Later that summer, I was informed that Reverend Mother wished to see me. After dinner, I went to her office, but there was a long line of Sisters who were there before me. Mother spent only one hour each evening speaking with Sisters who wanted to see her. After a bell rang, she didn't meet with anyone else, so everyone who was left in line just went to her recreation period that was already in progress.

I tried several times to meet with Reverend Mother, but the line of Sisters never dwindled. I finally realized that the nuns at the front of the line had skipped dinner, which was against the rules. Even though I knew it was wrong, I decided to try that method, too. It worked!

When I finally saw her, Mother asked me if I knew why I was there. Because I had previously experienced penances for so many infractions, I didn't want to incriminate myself by telling her something she might not even know about. Could it be having my picture taken?...having boys in my classroom? ... sleeping in chapel?... showing my feelings when my superior accused me of doing something I hadn't done? I figured it was probably because of having the boys in my classroom, but I told her I didn't know why I was there.

Mother became irritated and said I should think about it and come back to see her in two weeks when I could admit to my fault. I was concerned because I still wasn't sure *which* infraction she was talking about.

Two weeks later, I returned to Mother's office, as directed. She asked me again if I knew why I was there. I was nervous about mentioning any of my transgressions, so I repeated that I didn't know why I was there. She finally said, "What about the boys in your classroom?" I tried to explain the circumstances of these incidents, but she didn't want to listen. She said I had displeased Jesus, and I needed to make reparation to Him as soon as possible.

Although my meetings with Reverend Mother were disturbing, it was a sign of the times when young Sisters were taught to conform to all rules and regulations without question. This didn't daunt me. I knew God smiled on me, even when I made mistakes.

9

Chapter

MISSIONS: 1952-1955

1952–1953: St. Joseph and Ann School, New Mexico

It was extremely hot when we arrived in New Mexico. People were even frying eggs on the sidewalk. Since we were wearing our long woolen Habits, we were really feeling the heat. Fortunately, the convent was new, so it was air-conditioned; we had a reprieve from the heat when we were inside.

Sister Angela and I were both appointed to this school. That was disconcerting since our relationship in the novitiate had left much to be desired. When I mentioned this to Sister Caroline, our superior and principal, she said Sister Angela had already spoken to her about this matter. Apparently, she was just as apprehensive about our relationship as I was.

There were only nine of us in this convent, so differences with other Sisters were quite noticeable. Sister Angela and I were encouraged to make every effort to be civil to each other. Eventually, we actually became friend again.

I knew we were both scheduled to renew our vows in

January. This year, I should have taken mine for three years, but Reverend Mother didn't think I was worthy of that privilege; she allowed me to take them for only one year. This penance was particularly disturbing because I thought Sister Angela would be kneeling next to me when I professed my vows for only one year while she took hers for three. Sister Caroline assured me this was a moot issue because *both* of us would be taking our vows for only one year. I was astounded to hear that, because Sister Angela was always the "good" nun. What could she possibly have done to deserve this penance?

The next year, both Sister Angela and I were reassigned to New Mexico. We were both renewing our vows for two years, allowing us to "catch up" with our Band members who had already taken theirs for three years.

I was surprised to discover that prejudice was rampant in the state of New Mexico. While we were waiting for service in stores, the clerks often pretended they didn't see us. Men spit on us when we passed them. People crossed the street when they saw us. This was an eye-opener for me. I never realized nuns were not respected wherever we went.

Before school started in September, a list of children scheduled to be in each room was posted on the classroom door. While I was decorating my classroom, one mother came in to talk with me. After we'd talked for few minutes, she asked me if I was Indian. (My skin is dark.) I thought her question was odd; I soon discovered that Indian people were considered lower class in New Mexico. I told Sister Caroline about this conversation; she removed the little girl from my class and placed her in a room with an inexperienced teacher. When this mother asked why Sister Caroline changed the listing, Sister said, "If Sister Mary was Indian, you would have refused to have your daughter in her classroom. I wanted you to be sure your daughter wasn't getting an Indian teacher."

A performance of the *Passion Play* was scheduled at the Civic Center for all the Catholic schools. When our bus arrived, some principals were reboarding their students onto their own buses. The principals told us that when their children and teachers entered the building, the Indian children were placed in a separate line because they were to be seated in the balcony. The teachers said there was no way they'd attend this religious program under such a stipulation.

When more schools refused to let their children enter the building for this same reason, the program promoters apologized and said the Indian children would not be singled out; they could sit downstairs with the other children. Only then, did the teachers relent and allow their students to attend this program.

On the first Sunday of every month, we made a retreat. During that time, all superiors talked with Sisters who had not yet pronounced their final vows. *Good* and *not so good* issues were discussed. A report was then sent to Reverend Mother. When Sister Caroline spoke with me, she was always very kind. If I had been negligent about particular rules, she gently chided me and asked me to make a better effort the next month. She never made me feel like a bad person. In fact, she told me she never sent a negative report to the motherhouse.

When she was writing her thesis on Indian heritage, Sister Caroline often went to museums and historical sites for data. Sometimes I was privileged to accompany her and give her support by locating specific information for which she was searching. These were very special times for me because now I could give her assistance just as she always gave to me.

One morning at school, we heard a very loud rumble. The children fearfully looked up from their work. I assured them (as I believed) that a large truck had probably come down the street, causing the loud noise. We all went back to our tasks very calmly.

Shortly afterward, Sister Caroline arrived at my classroom door and asked if everyone was all right. I was puzzled by her question, so she explained that we had just experienced an earthquake.

Amazingly, the children trusted me enough to relax as I had directed. They remained composed and unafraid during the entire incident because of what I told them. Episodes like this made me realize my huge responsibility to protect the children under my care.

My mother traveled all the way to New Mexico to see me. Although our rules prevented her from eating with us, Sister Caroline made sure Mom received a tray in the parlor for each meal. She also allowed my mom to sleep in one of the empty convent bedrooms. Both my mother and I were extremely grateful for Sister's kindness.

One of our parishioners donated a TV set for us. It was situated in the parlor, so my mom used it while she waited for me during periods I couldn't be with her.   This was the *only* convent where I was stationed that Mom was treated so graciously. My mother stayed with us for three days. When she left, Mom went home lighthearted, not only because of the kindness she had received, but also because she knew Sister Caroline was a superior who appreciated each Sister – just as she was.

On Saturday evenings, we were allowed to watch Lawrence Welk, and sometimes, a National Geographic program on the new TV. Unfortunately, within the first year we had the TV, we received an edict from our higher superiors, indicating we were no longer allowed to use our TV sets. (However, one of our older Sisters, who ignored the rules about TV use, always rushed to see, as she called it, *Skip Along Hoppity* every Sunday afternoon.)

Regrettably, this "no TV" ruling was in force for three more years. I never understood why that privilege was taken from us when most nuns enjoyed only a few programs each week. I felt we were being treated like children who were told, "Do it because I said so."

New Mexico was a great mission. I was really unhappy when I was assigned elsewhere.

1954–1955: Presentation Academy, Illinois

At my next assignment, I was stationed where a new convent was being built. We taught at the parish school during the construction period, but for our living quarters, we stayed with other Sisters at a boarding school about a mile away. Since we walked back and forth from our parish school to the boarding school, we began looking for shortcuts.

We found that crossing a golf course saved us a great deal of time. Of course, the golfers didn't appreciate us interfering in their game. They often shouted obscenities at us, and they screamed that there was a path surrounding the golf course. We always thanked them pleasantly for this information, but we knew other golfers would be playing on other days, so we continued to use our shortcut until our new convent was built. As I look back, it must have been a remarkable sight to see seven nuns wearing full traditional Habits, traipsing across the golf course.

At the boarding school, we were each assigned an employment every morning. Mine was to clean the drawing rooms, so I went to the art studio to fulfill my duty. Sister Marie Anthony, the art director, said she didn't need any assistance; she asked who sent me there. When I told her the superior told me to clean the drawing rooms, she chuckled and told me the building was once a mansion and the downstairs parlors were still called *drawing rooms*. I thought, "If this building is now being used as a convent, why would the nuns continue to use terms that rich people had previously used?"

There was a lot of racial discrimination in our city: June left her arithmetic book home, so I told her she could sit with Sadie and share her book. When June didn't move, I told her again to go to Sadie's desk so she could complete her assignment. June still didn't move. She looked at me and said, "I don't sit with maids." Sadie was "colored." She looked at me and said, "That's OK. I'm used to it." It was hard to believe that children were being brought up to be so intolerant.

I saw a clerk giving change to a "colored" man. At that time, change was usually handed to the customer. Instead of putting his change in his hand, she threw it on the counter.

There was a city ordinance that no "colored" people were to be seen on *our* side of town after nine o'clock p.m. If they were caught, they would be arrested.

Since I was now stationed in Illinois, Jeanette and Ed, my younger sister and her husband, were able to visit me frequently. I always looked forward to seeing them; they usually brought their three delightful children with them.

Jeanette was incredibly artistic; she loved to create decorations for my home. She brought beautiful handmade bouquets of flowers for my tables and ornate needlepoint prints to hang on my living room walls. For her many friends, she decorated bottles and vases as unusual gifts. During May, the month dedicated to our Blessed Mother, she designed exquisite crowns for all the statues of Mary throughout the school.

Although she was ill, Jeanette created many other unique items. One of my favorites was the intricate earrings made of tiny shells. These were gifts for all the teachers. She also crafted picture frames and other jewelry, such as friendship bracelets and necklaces. No craft was too hard for her. I was the lucky recipient of many of her projects.

Ed helped their children plant a vegetable garden in their backyard. Tommy and Gerry each had their own section of the garden. Even Suzie, who was three-years old, had a little patch for herself. Ed showed them how to plant their seeds, and they all eagerly watched their plants grow. The best part of this project was picking the vegetables when they were full grown.

The children were delighted when they could bring baskets of food into their kitchen for cooking. Since this produce came from their own gardens, the kids ate vegetables they normally wouldn't touch. The children loved their garden project, but they also loved spending time with their dad.

Due to Jeanette's illness, she was unable to spend much time with the children, so Ed took them on adventures. Sometimes, Tommy and Gerry went on trips where Suzie was too young to join them. In that case, when they came home, Ed always spent extra time playing with Suzie. The two older children went to Navy Pier where they enjoyed the rides and carnival atmosphere; at street fairs they were entertained, not only by the incredible works of the artists, but also by the clowns, comedians, and mimes they met along the way. All three of the children went on other trips where Suzie could be included: parks, the beach, movies, and children's museums. They were always delighted when Ed proposed an outing with them.

Meanwhile, as an outreach to our nuns' parents, our Community superiors requested us to arrange a luncheon for those relatives who lived in the area. The idea was to create a source for parents to meet one another and provide them with a list of names so they could all stay in contact with one another. Some parents who came to the luncheon were delighted their daughter had selected the religious life, and they were also delighted to acquire a list of the other parents' names; other parents couldn't accept the fact that their daughter had given up her career, and in some cases, her fortune. These parents weren't the least bit interested in any list. They went home just as disgruntled as they were before they came.

My parents were a bit ambivalent. My father was very religious, and he was thrilled I'd entered the convent. My mother was still disappointed I hadn't gone into nursing, but she was always supportive of me.

The next day, our neighboring school was totally engulfed in a horrible fire. It was discovered that an eighth-grade boy had lit a large barrel of paper under a stairwell. More than a hundred children and nuns died in this terrible blaze—a tragedy that left everyone traumatized. The pastor had a nervous breakdown, and the parents of the deceased children expressed their sorrow in ways that ranged from acceptance to rage and anger at God.

Our children were terrified that such a thing might happen in our school. They didn't want to sit near warm radiators; they didn't even want to sit at desks where the warm sunshine brightened the classroom. Parents had numerous questions about our school's fire regulations.

Families were assured that intense safety precautions were

being adopted in all schools. Frequent fire drills, both announced and unannounced, were inaugurated by the fire department. The children learned that it was imperative to be silent during these drills in case a fireman gave them directions. Sometimes a fireman removed a child from the line and placed that child in a secluded area. This was a test to see if the teacher knew anyone was missing from the class. These same procedures were adopted throughout the country.

This was one of the most challenging incidents of my career. Parents and students were profoundly affected by this terrible tragedy. At that point, learning was secondary in their lives. Safety was predominant.

10
Chapter

PREPARATION AND PROFESSION OF FINAL VOWS

The year after our three-year vows were completed, our Band left our missions and returned to the motherhouse to prepare for our profession of final vows. Our prayer life was combined with physical duties, such as those we did as first-year novices: cleaning the chapel, washing windows, helping in the infirmary, working in the laundry, scrubbing floors, and assisting in any way that was needed.

One of our major requirements during this period was to make a thirty-day retreat. Our retreat was presented by our new Reverend Mother, a very saintly person. We had group meditations with her twice each day. She also met with us individually to discuss our decision to dedicate our lives to God forever. She made every effort to be sure we were fully informed of all the implications involved, and that we understood we were making a binding promise to God. Profound Silence was obligatory so we could more easily stay focused on our future lives. Thirty days! I never thought I could be quiet that long.

One afternoon, Sister Mary Patricia and I were silently washing dishes in the infirmary. She dropped a dish, but I caught it. That caused us to giggle uncontrollably. We started throwing more dishes to each other while we were still laughing. When we looked up, Reverend Mother was standing in the kitchen doorway. She didn't say anything to us, but she looked very disappointed.

At our next group meditation, Mother announced that some of us didn't seem to be taking the retreat seriously. Both Sister Mary Patricia and I apologized to her. She didn't give us any reparation to perform; she said our disappointment with ourselves was enough of a penance.

On Transition Day, our Band of twelve pronounced our final vows during an impressive ceremony. Just as before, postulants were outfitted in wedding gowns and they received their Holy Habits. Other Sisters took their first vows; and others renewed their vows for three years. Finally, we were called forth to publicly announce that we were ready to serve God for the rest of our lives.

I made my vows, fully intending to keep them forever. However, twenty-eight years later, when the world was changing, I felt compelled to change with it.

After all the ceremonies were over, Reverend Mother invited our Band to a special luncheon. She had arranged to have this surprise in a room she reserved just for us. We were delighted that she joined us. I don't remember what we ate; the food didn't matter. Reverend Mother had provided us with a loving commemoration of the thirty days we had just spent with her.

The next day, we left for our missions. I replaced a Sister who was returning to the motherhouse to prepare for her final vows.

11
Chapter

~

MISSIONS: 1956–1966

1956: Peace and Serenity School, Wisconsin

This assignment was at a small school in Wisconsin. We had only four Sisters, so we took turns cooking dinner. Those whose turn it was to cook left immediately after school to make preparations for the meal.

Billy, one of my first-graders, had acted up throughout the day. Since I was cooking that evening, I told him he had to stay after school and come to the convent with me. As soon as I told him he'd be coming to the convent, he began crying hysterically.

Children were frequently brought to the convent for various reasons, so I was startled by his strong reaction. I learned later that a playground rumor had been circulated about the nuns having a spanking machine in the convent. Billy was terrified it would be used on him.

While our food was in the oven, I decided to make some copies of worksheets for my class. As soon as I started the copier, Billy began screaming, "I'll be good! I promise I'll be good!"

This poor child was convinced I was preparing the spanking machine for him. It took a long time to calm him down.

He kept asking if it was *for real* that we didn't have a spanking machine. I tried to persuade him that the rumor was untrue. I even had him help me retrieve the worksheets from the copier so he could see how the machine was used. He was still dubious, so I showed him there was no way he'd fit inside the copier. He was finally convinced he had escaped a terrible experience.

On Thanksgiving Day, it was my turn to cook again. Everything went well: the mashed potatoes were smooth; the vegetables were perfect; the layered Jell-O salad was a picture; and the turkey looked great. However, since I'd never carved a turkey, I should have asked for help. I really messed it up! Instead of nice slices, there were only chunks of meat. No one complained, but I felt terrible. In my pride, I wanted everything to be perfect.

My superior was young and fun to be with; she wasn't at all strict about rules. She allowed us to speak during dinner almost every evening; she always left a bowl of candy on the community room table; she let us listen to *Mr. and Mrs. North* (a radio program) during our study periods; and she left personal items like toothpaste, hand cream, talcum powder, deodorant, combs, and hairbrushes in an open cabinet where we could help ourselves without asking permission. She was also quite lax about meeting with us on retreat Sundays. Following her example, none of us practiced Profound Silence very well. We sometimes carried on conversations well into the night.

That year was the seventy-fifth anniversary of the parish. The parish ladies provided a festive dinner for all the priests and nuns in town. Reverend Mother and all her assistants attended this banquet. We were astonished when Mother said, "I see wine glasses on the table. Shouldn't they be filled?" Of course we were all delighted, since alcohol was ordinarily strictly forbidden.

There were other small schools in our town, and we frequently had get-togethers with their Sisters. I looked forward to these meetings because we always exchanged classroom ideas and discussed new projects with one another. We made arrangements for our classes to go on field trips together; we had competitions with science and art projects; and friendly rivalries took place in after-school activities.

The parish families loved the nuns; they frequently brought casseroles and desserts for us. They also drove us to the national park and points of interest in the city. It seemed they couldn't do enough for us.

The children were well-mannered, their assignments were almost always completed, and there were very few discipline problems. I couldn't ask for better parental cooperation. They believed in the old axiom, "If you get in trouble at school, you'll be in more trouble at home."

I resented rigidity, but I was troubled with our extremely lax way of living. Even so, I was dismayed when I was transferred again. I had no confidence that I was being accepted by my colleagues, and I figured they probably wanted to make sure I didn't return to live with them.

I was getting discouraged, but I never doubted that God was right there with me.

1957: National Elementary School, Illinois

One summer, I was assigned to teach English as a Second Language to eight Hispanic children. I genuinely enjoyed teaching these courteous youngsters who were eager to learn

English. They were always on time for their classes, and they never failed to do their assignments.

We spent part of each morning interacting with one another in English. Sometimes, when the students needed help, I tried to explain the issue to them in Spanish. However, I knew very little Spanish, so they enjoyed it when I made language errors. It proved to them that learning another language is difficult for everyone.

I took these youngsters on some field trips where they had delightful reactions to everything they experienced. We went to a museum, the beach, and a restaurant. The only rule was: they were required to speak English on these excursions.

By the end of the summer, most of these youngsters had gained a lot of fluency with speaking and writing English. On the last day of class, they expressed their gratitude by presenting me with handmade cards written in English, and their parents sent some Hispanic desserts. Since these young people realized they would now be more successful in school because of their new language skills, they were eager to return to their regular classes. This group of students was a teacher's dream!

That summer, the other Sisters who were staying in that same convent were assigned various duties: teaching math and reading in summer school classes, assisting children to select appropriate library books, or organizing children's activities in the park. I think I had the best assignment of all!

One evening, five of us decided to go for a walk. We suddenly realized we were very near one of the professional baseball parks. We walked over there and convinced the caretaker to let us in to see the grounds. We were wearing our traditional long Habits, so once we were in the park, we pinned up our skirts and started running around the bases. We went into the dugout;

we pretended we were pitching a ball; we stood in the outfield; and we imagined we were the catcher.

Meanwhile, the caretaker was "beside himself." He realized what a big mistake he'd made by letting us into the grounds. He tried his best to get us to leave, but we were having so much fun that we were reluctant to listen to him. We had no concept that this poor man could have lost his job if anyone had seen us. Thank goodness no reporters happened to be around.

1958–1959: Our Lady of Fatima School, Minnesota

I had a delightful first-grade class. There was no problem with parental cooperation. In fact, the parents were frequently at my door, asking how they could help me. This was a school where I felt greatly appreciated.

Sometimes my allergy caused me to sneeze very loudly exactly seven times. I told the children it was polite to say, "God bless you" when someone sneezed, so the next time it happened, I could see the little ones counting my sneezes. When I reached "seven," they all called out in unison, "God bless you, Sister!"

Some of the other classrooms had their doors open, so they heard my children blessing me in their singsong way. When I sneezed again, youngsters from several classes called out, "God bless you, Sister," together with my class. This little occurrence always provided an opportunity for the children and their teachers to have a little chuckle.

One afternoon, Lily, one of my first-graders, did something wrong, I wanted to impress on her that what she did was very naughty, so I sent her to Sister Marie George's eighth-grade classroom. The older youngsters loved the little ones, so when Lily arrived, they were all ready to enjoy her. Their class had a chart indicating stars for good achievement and green squares for those who needed improvement. When Lily tried to explain what she had done, Sister Marie George turned to her class and *solemnly* asked what they thought Lily's punishment should be. Someone called out, "Give her a green square," so Sister Marie George pasted a green square sticker on Lily's forehead.

When she returned to our classroom, Lily was crying hysterically. I tried to find out why she was so upset, but she just kept saying, "Green square!" I had no idea what that meant, but Lily was certainly affected by it.

After I learned the meaning of "green square," I discussed it with the children in my class. They understood that misbehavior would be handled by making a "visit" to Sister Marie George's classroom to get one of those green squares. This was a great deterrent to making bad choices.

At this school, the children were required to attend Mass before school started each morning. Most of the first-graders were bored during the Service, so they concocted various ways to entertain themselves. One morning, Joseph decided to crawl under the benches and bite Matthew's ankle. Naturally, Matthew screamed, and there was quite a commotion in church.

The nuns from the other classes tried to keep their students from laughing, but they weren't very successful. Not too many children or teachers had their minds on the Mass that was in progress. When I asked Joseph why he did that, he responded, "Because I wanted to." Of course, when we returned to our classroom, he was sent upstairs to get a terrible green square.

An incident of a different kind involved Norman. He overheard a conversation at home about his mother being critically ill, and there wasn't much hope she would survive. When his father brought him to school, Norman absolutely refused to enter the building. He wanted to be home with his mother, not at school. His father and I talked with him about the importance of school; we told him we knew his mother would want him there. He didn't care. He just wanted to be with her.

Norman's father tried everything he could think of to coerce his son to return to school. He even called the police station to see if any of the police officers would talk to Norman. A very kind sergeant agreed to do so, but Norman wouldn't listen to him. Norman said they could take him to jail, but he wasn't going to school. He just wanted to stay with his mom.

Since Norman wouldn't return to school, his father hired a tutor to work with him at home so he wouldn't get too far behind in his classwork. Norman spent many hours at his mother's bedside.

After three months, Norman's mother *did* recuperate, but he still wouldn't leave her side. We found a solution. Although his mother was still very weak, she sat in the back of our classroom where he could see her. That worked just fine because he could go back and hug her any time he wanted to be cuddled. When he was more secure that she wasn't "going away," his mother stood outside the school for a little while where he could see her through the classroom window.

Ordinarily, the children who lived close to school walked home for lunch by themselves. However, even though Norman lived only a block away, his mother understood his need to be assured that she was all right; she came to pick him up for lunch; she came again when he was dismissed from school in the afternoon. Little by little, Norman began participating in class activities again. When he was confident his mom would be there for him, he was finally able to be a little boy again. His love for his mother outweighed any penalties he might incur.

I loved this school, and I was very disappointed when I was transferred again. I had a hard time accepting this as the Will of God. Some of the parents asked if there was anything they could do to keep me there. I appreciated their concern, but I knew their efforts would be futile.

1960: St. Bernard Academy, Wisconsin

I was assigned to this school with Sister Veronica, a nun I loved. She had been taken out of the classroom and confined to the motherhouse infirmary for many years because she was told the scar on her face (from cancer surgery) was too horrid for others to see. Consequently, she wasn't allowed to mingle with the other Sisters or the schoolchildren. Yet, when the baby boomers came along, more nuns were needed in the schools, so she was brought out of her isolation and placed in a second-grade classroom. This *cruelty* was almost unbelievable!

Her stomach churned daily as she tried to be obedient. Since she was told previously she was too ugly to associate with other Sisters or children, how could she expect children or their parents to tolerate her? Even when she spoke to the Sisters in the convent, she always turned her head away from them so no one would need to look at her "repulsive" face.

My heart ached for Sister Veronica. She had no self-confidence or self-esteem; she had no desire to stand up for herself. She was one of the most spiritual nuns I ever knew. I admired her and wanted to spend as much time as possible with her.

After school, Sister Veronica always retired to her bedroom to prepare her classes and spend time in prayer. I frequently visited her there so we could talk and pray together. Since what we were doing was somewhat private, I closed her bedroom door—which was an infraction of the rules.

Later, at a Community meeting, one Sister brought up

the fact that Sister Veronica and I were talking behind closed doors. (This usually implied that gossip about other Sisters or Community rules was being discussed.) All the Sisters were reminded that talking behind closed doors was an infraction of the rules.

Sister Veronica, who was very frail, became extremely upset when the nuns claimed she had done something wrong; she left the room in tears. Because she was so sensitive, and she had so little self-esteem, this accusation caused her to become very ill. She was confined to her bed for three days. Needless to say, our little meetings were over. Both of us were devastated because we had profited so much from this spiritual friendship.

During Sister Veronica's recuperation, she was too ill to eat anything; however, meal trays were still brought to her, and it was my privilege to bring them to her. However, she told me to have someone else bring them because she didn't want me to get in trouble for talking to her. At that point, all I cared about was Sister Veronica. (After I left the convent, the only time I returned to the motherhouse was to visit Sister Veronica when she was critically ill.)

This was the year that modified Habits were approved for any Sister who wished to make the change from her traditional Habit. Of course, Sister Veronica didn't want to replace her Habit because, not only was she steeped in Community traditions, she knew the new Habit would show more of her face. She felt even more isolated when every Sister in our convent replaced her traditional Habit with the new garb.

Sister Veronica knew I was extremely involved in parish activities. Although she never understood why I wanted to participate in every project, she always supported me.

Our pastor enjoyed presenting musical plays; I directed the music for them. This was frowned upon, but my higher superiors reluctantly gave me permission to do this because Father convinced them he couldn't produce plays without my assistance.

These plays were big-city events! It was incredible to see the number of people who came for auditions. We always found several talented individuals for the roles we needed.

We spent approximately three hours at each evening rehearsal. Many times the cast and crew went out for pizza afterward; on those nights I returned to the convent quite late. Some of the Sisters made comments about this. It was even suspected that only the pastor and I went out together. When I heard this, I responded, "Yes, Father and I went out together— *with eight other people.*" I prayed daily that I could love and forgive these Sisters who questioned my integrity.

One of the musicals we performed that year was *Fiddler on the Roof.* Father took the part of Tevya, and for the most part, he did very well. However, sometimes he forgot his lines and just made up something else. Sometimes he repeated parts of a song, and sometimes he skipped sections of the music. The actors and musicians were incredible—they just followed along as if that's the way things were meant to be. Unless someone in the audience was extremely familiar with the score, no one would realize anything was amiss.

The other play that year was *The King and I.* Father decided that *I* would be his choice for the part of Lady Thiang, the king's head wife. At first my superiors rejected this plan. However, after Father had many discussions with them, I was given the permission to perform. Little did they know my costume entailed a long, sleeveless dress; lots of makeup; and a hairpiece entwined with pearls.

Since the performances were on two weekends, and the hairpiece was difficult to rework, I wore it all week: to school, in the chapel, and during meals. This didn't faze the schoolchildren, but the nuns had a lot to say about it. (I have no idea why we didn't use a wig.)

The first time I appeared on stage, I could hear whispers throughout the audience, "That's Sister!" It was a little daunting, because people had only seen me wearing my modified Habit. Now I was costumed as Lady Thiang, and I was totally out of my religious element. However, I knew I performed well. The audience loved it, and Father was well pleased. Some of my superiors were in the front row of the auditorium. None of them ever made any comment to me about my performance.

This was one of the schools where I was told I was too friendly with the pastor who was trying to involve the community in parish activities. My participation in his projects gave concern to my superiors, so I was relocated again. At least I knew why I was being transferred this time, but I was dismayed that my integrity was being questioned. I knew I couldn't do anything about this transfer, so I just harbored my disappointment, dissatisfaction, and frustration in my heart.

1961: Our Lady of the World School, Illinois

While I was stationed at this convent, my father had a severe stroke. One of our rules was "no home visits," so I was unable to visit my dad who was bedridden. He was asking for me and sulking when my mom told him I couldn't come to see him. In desperation, Mom finally called my superior and asked if there was any way my visit could be arranged.

After the higher superiors finally approved this request, I was given permission to be with my dad for a half-hour each week, with a companion. (Fortunately, my companion was a lively nun who my father liked a lot.) Since we weren't allowed to drive at that time, I was grateful that one of our parishioners kindly drove us each week.

My mother said the only time Dad was happy was when I was there. He always cried when it was time for me to leave. My heart was heavy as I walked to the door and left him sobbing.

It had been eighteen years since I'd left home. I was astounded when I saw that my parents were actually living close to poverty. The furniture, wallpaper, and carpets had been old when I left for the Community. These were still there, only now they were *older*. The windows needed washing, the cracked glass needed to be repaired, the grass needed cutting, there were watermarks on the ceiling, and several repairs were crucial. There was no one to help my parents, so there was a lot of deterioration in the house.

When I saw how they were living, I was embarrassed to realize I was actually living in the lap of luxury. The parishioners always made sure the nuns had the finest of everything: silverware, gorgeous dishes, delicate glassware, electric blankets in every room, colored TVs on every floor, and so much more. Dad's blanket was frayed at the top. Blankets like this were discarded in our convent.

I never realized how financially difficult it was for my parents to visit me wherever I was stationed. Since my dad was now incapacitated, my mom came alone. She never mentioned anything about their finances, and I didn't ever think to ask. I'd felt very free to ask my mom to purchase sterling silver medals and holy cards, so I could use them for children's prizes.

Anything I wanted or needed was sent to me immediately. I was deprived of nothing. Yet my parents sacrificed everything so they could make me happy. I took the vow of poverty, but they were certainly living it. That was a sad lesson for me.

A terrible family tragedy occurred that year. Jeanette and Ed's two older children, Tommy and Gerry, contracted chickenpox. Suzie, their youngest daughter, didn't show any signs of the disease, but she became very ill. Jeanette and Ed put her to bed, but during the night they heard her scream. When they ran to her, she was unconscious. They rushed her to the hospital emergency room.

The doctor said she had a very serious illness, encephalitis, which was related to chickenpox; hers invaded the inside of her body. Suzie was admitted to the hospital, but she died the next day. Jeanette and Ed were devastated. My sister became hysterical, and Ed moaned as he sat in a chair. He was so affected by Suzie's death that years afterward he could never talk about her. If her name came up in conversation, he had to leave the room.

It was up to me to inform my parents about Suzie's death. The minute my mother opened the door, she said, "She's gone, isn't she!" When I told her it was true, Mom leaned against the wall, slumped to the floor, and started to cry uncontrollably. My father, who was bedridden, also sobbed. He said, "Why didn't God take me instead of her?"

Since Jeanette and Ed lived in a suburb, Suzie was waked at a suburban funeral home. They told me a net had been placed over her casket because her chickenpox was finally exposed, and her body was covered with lesions.

One of our teachers, Miss Johnson, volunteered to bring me to the wake. Sister Eloise, our principal and superior, reluctantly gave me permission to attend the wake. She said that since it was such a long distance away, she was concerned I wouldn't make it back in time for afternoon prayers. She thought the traffic would probably be too heavy! I couldn't believe my ears. Sisters often missed afternoon prayers for various reasons.

When we were on our way to the funeral home, a huge snowstorm developed. For safety reasons, Miss Johnson had to turn back and we returned home.

Jeanette and Ed had planned to have Suzie's funeral two days later, but Sister Eloise said I couldn't attend until Saturday— four days later, when we were out of school. Consequently, the date for Suzie's funeral was changed so I could be there. This regulation didn't sit well with my family because it meant that Suzie's body was laid out for almost a week. By Saturday, parts of her body were shriveling.

It was hard for me to believe how unsympathetic Sister Eloise was to such a tragedy. Surely my classroom could have been covered for one day so I could attend Suzie's funeral earlier in the week. I didn't tell Sister Eloise how resentful I felt because respect for authority was ingrained in me. But was this really the way God wanted us to handle circumstances like this? I realized I was following old rules and I was having a hard time accepting them.

Meanwhile, my mother purchased a little VW and took driving lessons. She needed the car because she didn't want to leave Dad alone for too long while she went to get his prescriptions and did her shopping. Previously, she had walked to the stores and carried all the groceries home, but now that was too difficult for her.

Unfortunately, Mom wasn't a good driver; she usually took both lanes on the road. When bus or truck drivers honked at her, she'd say, "Just because they're bigger than I am, they think I'm going to move for them!"

Just when Mom and Dad were getting used to the rule where I could visit my dad for short periods each week, I was told I'd be transferring again. Despite the fact that my father was ill, this time I would be going to a distant school. I was resentful because of my family circumstances. I didn't know how to express my displeasure because my feelings were of anger, and that was not allowed. I felt rebellious but I didn't know how to handle it.

1962–1963: Infant of Prague School, California

Because of my family situation, I was astounded when I was assigned to a school in California. My parents were devastated. I saw them before I left for my new mission, and both of them were sobbing. I told them I had special permission to call them regularly, but that didn't soothe their feelings. My dad said, "Maybe this is the last time I'll see you. Maybe I'll be dead before you see me again." It was *very* difficult to leave them that afternoon.

I went to my new mission in California with a heavy heart, but I was delighted when I saw that our convent and school were surrounded by all the beauty of nature, especially the majestic mountains. Saturday was cleaning day when we scrubbed floors, scoured bathrooms, cleaned cabinets, polished silverware, washed clothes, and cleaned windows. I always volunteered to clean the windows because this was my opportunity to watch the clouds roll *up* the mountains. I was totally fascinated by this phenomenon. Because of all this natural beauty, I felt more spiritual and closer to God than at any other time in my life.

Sometimes one of our parishioners offered to drive us to the mountains. One gentleman who chauffeured us had a bad habit of turning around to respond to something we said. Since there were lots of hairpin turns on the mountain, it was nerve-wracking when he wasn't watching the road. The next time he drove, we all decided that no one would talk so he wouldn't get distracted.

We always had a great time in the mountains. It wasn't really cold, so we built snowmen, threw snowballs, made snow forts, and thoroughly enjoyed the experience. We always piled snow on top the car because when we returned to the city, children met us and asked if they could play with the snow.

Another parishioner took three of us to Disneyland. We loved the attractions, the rides, and all the Disney characters walking around the grounds. Although Sister Martha, our superior, had permitted us to go on this adventure, she was appalled when we told her we had actually ridden on some of the rides and attended several side shows. (We weren't quite sure what she thought we'd be doing there.)

Due to heavy traffic, we were late for dinner. Since this was a silent meal, it seemed to be a serious misdemeanor. However, that didn't change any part of the delightful afternoon we'd had.

Because I was so far away from my family, some of the Sisters who lived in a convent near my parents asked for permission to visit them in my absence. Dad was so happy to see them that he even tried to get up to play his piano again Sister Michelle was a violinist, so she always brought her instrument with her. She accompanied Dad while he tried to play the piano. I was very grateful for the kindness and thoughtfulness of these nuns. They brought a lot of joy to my dad when I couldn't be there. That was true sisterly love.

It was getting increasingly more difficult for Dad to press down the piano keys, so he became discouraged. However, my mother purchased an electric organ for him where the keys were easier to play. I was fortunate to eventually obtain the organ in a roundabout way. It is presently in my home.

(When Dad knew he was dying, he made it clear that, because the nuns had been so good to him, he wanted them to have his organ. They appreciated this gift and made good use of it. However, several years later when the convent was being demolished, everything was being sold or given away. One of the nuns, who remembered that my dad had donated the organ to them, kindly contacted me and asked if I would like to have it. I appreciated her thoughtfulness and made arrangements to have it delivered to my apartment in Chicago, where I was living at the time.)

Celebrating Christmas in California was inspiring. The altar in our chapel was decorated with flowers from our own backyard. Although our midnight Mass was nothing like what they experienced at the motherhouse, its simplicity was exceptionally uplifting.

There was no gift exchange, of course, but Sister Martha put a huge box of chocolates on the community room table for us. We had our dinner outside on picnic tables because it was so sunny and warm. Some Sisters missed the freezing weather and snow "up north," but I didn't miss it at all.

I called my parents to wish them a Merry Christmas. They were happy to hear from me, but they were sad I couldn't be with them. My dad started crying, and by the time I finished the call, I was crying, too.

Our school enrollment was exceptionally high because there were still lots of baby boomers across the country. I had seventy-two children in my first-grade class, but I was able to manage them myself. God had to be my co-pilot because I could have never done that alone.

In order to teach the children on their own level, I set up seven different reading groups; each one had a special color assigned to it. Every day a leader was selected from each group. While I was teaching reading to a small section of the class, each leader checked the work of the other children in the group.

If the assignment was completed correctly, the leader stamped the paper and the child was allowed to do extra credit papers, "cook" in the play kitchen, use the rocking chair, or work with grammar exercises on the blackboard.

Surprisingly, the grammar exercises were the children's favorite choice. Colored envelopes, with skills for each group, were taped on the wall below the blackboard. It was exciting to see how well each group progressed. (Some of the more advanced children learned to use punctuation marks: commas, question marks, and quotation marks.)

Sometimes the leaders were stricter than I would have been. If a child was just a speck off the line of a writing paper, the leader would quietly show the child what was wrong by pointing to the error. The child was then required to correct the error to the leader's satisfaction.

Homework sheets for each group were sent home daily. These explained to the parents what new words their children learned that day. These words were to be reviewed each evening to solidify the children's understanding of their new vocabulary. Due to wonderful parental cooperation, the next day the children in each group were usually ready to move on to the next section of their book.

Judith, one of my first-graders, was having difficulty seeing the blackboard. I suggested to her mother that she might need her eyes examined. They did go to an optometrist, and Judith's mother was devastated when she found that her beautiful little girl would need glasses. She said her daughter wouldn't look so lovely anymore if she wore them. I was appalled that she placed so much emphasis on outward beauty.

Not surprisingly, Judith's mother ordered eight pairs of glasses for her. Each one was a different color so Judith would be color-coordinated every day. I was sorry this mother presumed that glasses would destroy her child's beauty, despite the fact she could see better and her grades were improving.

Because our class was so large, and the children were eager to tell me things throughout the day, I set aside a daily "special listening time" when they could tell me something interesting about a personal incident. However, sometimes I had to cut them off when they were describing family quarrels or other personal family issues. Most of the time they talked about accomplishments and amusing experiences they had with their younger siblings: watching babies laugh when they stumbled as they were learning to walk; being disgusted when babies were so messy when they ate; feeling amused when their siblings chose unmatched clothing to wear; and having a little sister run to a man she *thought* was her father.

One child described searching the house for his little brother. They found him sleeping with the new puppy. Another child called 911, and the police actually came to their home. An expensive incident occurred when a sibling was playing with the telephone and dialed an overseas number. There were many more stories, such as youngsters eating fish from the fishbowl and parents taking snapshots of their children when they were hugging and kissing each other.

I loved the honesty and innocence of these children. Their eyes sparkled when they spoke. Parents told me their children loved school, and they couldn't wait to come each day. I couldn't wait to get there either.

After school, many of the parents talked to me about their child's progress. They were very generous in offering their assistance for various projects. I utilized their services in many ways, especially for checking papers and preparing materials for art classes. Some parents even volunteered to work with small groups of children in my classroom.

During the summer, since we didn't return to the motherhouse, we took classes where some of the nuns ordinarily taught high school. I particularly loved the classes taught by Sister Monica: literature and creative writing. She motivated me to read several classics not required, and I wrote a number of short stories. She encouraged me to keep writing. She said I had a gift, and it was important for me to develop it. She was one of the best teachers I ever had—a true inspiration!

When we went back to school, I had sixty-nine children on my list. Since last year's schedule worked so well, I prepared activities that would help me achieve the same success this year. Again, the parents were extremely cooperative, and the children never wanted to miss school, even when they were ill.

At the end of that school year, I was told I was being transferred again. I knew I had done a good job in my classroom, and teachers who observed my class gave me high praise. However, even though my transfer would bring me closer to my parents, I was distraught because I was being assigned to teach *eighth grade*!

I could hardly control my resentment! How sad it was that my superiors took a good teacher from the primary grades to become a mediocre one in the upper grades. (Sadly, I was never again assigned to teach primary grades.)

I was expected to believe this was done in my best interests, but I had a very hard time accepting this decision. What were my best interests? Who was taking the responsibility for deciding what they were? Were my feelings ever involved? Yes, I felt rebellious!

1964: Dominican Academy, Illinois

At my new assignment, where I was required to teach eighth grade, I had no problem instructing the students in English or language arts. However, since it had been so long since I studied social studies and math, I needed extra preparation time for those subjects—especially since the schools were now teaching *modern math.*

One of our Community rules was to have our bedroom lights out by nine o'clock p.m. However, because of my inability to complete my lesson plans in the allotted time, I often disobeyed this rule and kept preparing for my next day's classes after the curfew. Sometimes, when I was working past the deadline, Sister Marie Anthony, our superior, came to my room and shut off the light. At these times, I went to bed crying because I knew I wasn't ready for forty-eight eighth-grade students the next day.

Our new Reverend Mother was one of the nuns who taught me in high school. I thought if I went to the motherhouse and explained my dilemma, she would understand and give me the permission I needed to prepare my classes properly. I was astonished when she said, "You have a vow of obedience, so you should get to bed on time. *God* will help you in your classroom." I knew that wouldn't work, so I continued studying past the curfew whenever I needed to do so. Of course, Reverend Mother was informed.

Some of the parishioners thought I'd get brownie points if they told Sister Marie Anthony they knew I worked hard because they saw my bedroom light on many evenings. I cringed every time they tried to help me. There were no brownie points!

A few years before my dad's strokes, he made a beautiful tape of his piano playing. I knew he liked to hear me sing, so on Sunday afternoons I often went to my classroom to make tapes for him. I used two tape recorders: one to record his music and the other to record my singing with his music.

One Sunday afternoon I didn't complete my tape because I had to leave for afternoon prayers. When I returned to my classroom, both recorders were missing. I was really upset. The recorders were gone, and my father's tape was on one of them.

I hoped that whoever took the recorders would brag about the theft so we would have some idea of who stole them. The next day, I asked all the students in my eighth-grade class to write an anonymous note saying they didn't know anything about the robbery, or that someone they knew was involved. The notes provided information about two boys who had broken into the school and stolen the equipment.

Sister Marie Anthony and I met with the boys and their parents. The recorders were recovered, but unfortunately, the boys had erased the tape. My dad's recording was irreplaceable. What a huge disappointment!

I was very naïve about sexual behavior of teens, so when some of the girls complained that the boys were making "signs" at them, I asked, "What kind of signs?" They said they were too embarrassed to show me. Since I had no idea what the girls were talking about, I tried watching the boys, but I never saw any indication they were doing anything wrong.

The girls continued to complain, so I kept a few of them after school, and I insisted they show me the signs they were talking about. Finally, two girls reluctantly illustrated some of them. Afterward, I watched for these actions with the boys, but I'm sorry to admit I seldom saw' the signs that were so offensive to the girls.

On the whole, I detested teaching this age level a lot. I especially disliked the attitude of some students; most of them disliked me too. It was a penance for me to fulfill the work that God apparently expected of me. Teenage psychology was far different from that of little children, who were innocent and anxious to learn.

All students were required to attend daily Mass. The older youngsters "acted out" during the Mass. When Marion was reading *Elvis Presley* and *The Beatles* magazines, I took them away from her and kept them in my desk for the day. Others in the class wrote notes to one another and started giggling in church. Some drew pictures on their notebooks and passed them down the pew for others to see. They were no model for the younger children!

Toward the end of the year, eighth-graders were given blue and gold class ribbons which they proudly wore on their uniforms. However, all those who committed an offense had to put their ribbons on the bulletin board and leave them there for a few days.

Marion was well-liked, but she took chances, and she usually got caught. She shared her extra copies of *Elvis Presley* and *The Beatles* magazines during class time; during the lunch period, she and some friends rearranged the classroom furniture; and she helped others with their tests. By the time her class graduated Marion's ribbons were still very clean because they had spent more time on the bulletin board than on her uniform.

Despite my misery with these teenagers, it was a gift to get to know Marion better. She frequently came to school with bruises on various parts of her body. When I questioned her, she always had excuses: she bumped into a door… she fell down the stairs … her brothers accidentally hit her when they were playing together. She denied there were any serious family issues, but after I continued to probe and she began to trust me, she finally admitted that her father, who she loved, beat her when he was intoxicated. She knew he would apologize later, so she readily forgave him each time.

I was blessed to become Marion's mentor. However, because of our rules, I could advise her, but I couldn't get involved with her struggles. What a sad indictment for those of us who gave our lives and love to God so we could help those in need. Nevertheless, it was important to Marion that I cared about her and loved her. I prayed she would survive her terrible home situation and fulfill her dream of becoming a nurse, which she eventually did. No matter what was going on in her life, *Marion never gave up on God.*

Even though Marion struggled with family and personal issues, she always made sure I was all right. She stayed in touch with me, even when I was transferred from school to school. She also supported me when I was determining whether or not I would remain in the Community. She made me part of her life, and she is my best friend today.

Once again, at the end of the school year, I was transferred. Why? Even though I detested working with teenagers, I knew I'd given my heart and soul to do the best I could with them.

Yes, I was unhappy with teaching eighth grade, but I would have been very content to be assigned to another grade in the same school. I was distraught when I was transferred again. It seemed I wasn't wanted anywhere I went.

1965: St. Cecilia School, Ohio

My sixth-grade class at St. Cecilia's was amazing! They were well mannered, and they were children who would make their parents proud. They decorated the room, cleaned cabinets, and straightened out bookshelves without being told. When I expressed my gratitude and said how pleased I was with their effort, they tried even harder to make me happy.

Our teacher/student relationship was extraordinary. We could have fun together, but the children always showed nothing but respect for me. I thanked God daily for allowing me to have this reprieve from previous unpleasant situations.

After lunch, I tried to come out to the playground early. The children pleaded with me to bring them inside where they could practice some plays they had written. They really enjoyed working together on these projects. Some of their plays were very good; they even had commercials. It was a delight for me to be with them because they thoroughly enjoyed their school experience that year.

I was really *touched* when I received a letter from the children on my feast day. I can hardly read it, even today, without crying. I have saved it for over fifty years, and each time I read it, my heart jumps for joy.

> *Sister, you are celebrating your Feast Day today!*
> *We, your loving students, are very pleased and*
> *proud to help you celebrate it.*
> *We have never had a kinder Teacher than you,*
> *and we may not have one as kind ever again.*
> *Happy Feast Day, Dear Sister.*
> *May God bless you on this day*
> *and every day of your life.*
> *—The Students of Room 205*

This letter has always been comforting to me, especially during days that weren't quite so happy.

Another joyful day was the celebration of my twenty-fifth anniversary as a nun. The parish went "all out" for me. There was a Mass on Saturday afternoon where some of the choir members prepared exceptional music selections, and Father's homily *(sermon)* was all about the many things I'd done for the parish. I was so honored with all the preparation that went into this celebration.

After Mass I received a special blessing, and everyone proceeded to the auditorium where a catered sit-down dinner was served. Everyone from the parish had been invited to attend, at no charge. Although they were supposed to RSVP, extra tables were set up for those who might have forgotten to send in their response. Everyone was welcome! More than a hundred people attended this celebration.

But wait! There was more! Besides the delicious dinner, entertainment was provided in the form of skits, music, and speeches – all pertaining to me and my parish activities. I was overwhelmed by the love and gratitude shown to me. However, I also felt somewhat guilty because I had already started to consider leaving my Community.

This was definitely a good year for me. Having a loving class was a gift far beyond my dreams. I couldn't wait to get to school each day. I was more relaxed now, and my prayer life was obviously enhanced.

Sister Augusta was a wonderful superior. She made each of us feel special. I was surprised when she selected me to be the chapel sacristan. Since I had never been given this privilege before, I didn't even know how to lay out the priests' vestments; Sister Augusta kindly showed me how to do it.

When I asked her why she trusted me with this responsibility, Sister Augusta replied, "I knew you could do it, and I wanted to give you a chance!"

Of course, being a people-pleaser, I did everything I could to make good on this opportunity. Since I'd never had so much responsibility at any other convent, I was elated. I felt very special.

Once there was a negative occurrence in the convent, and Sister Augusta presumed I'd caused it. I was devastated because I knew I hadn't done it, but I couldn't excuse myself. When she discovered her error, she was in tears when she came to my bedroom during Profound Silence to apologize. It was unheard of that a superior would ever apologize to another Sister! My estimation of her went even higher.

I was so happy. My class was wonderful; my superior was the greatest; and all the nuns worked together as a team. Unfortunately, I wasn't destined to stay at this school another year. Why? If only I could question these transfers! I was doing so well at this school! Surely my colleagues didn't find me unsuitable to interact with them. Why?

I greatly resented this transfer. I wanted to speak up to my superiors, but I was still saddled with respect for authority. Although I was angry, I did what they demanded, just because I had taken a vow of obedience—and they said so.

Despite the fact that I felt rebellious, I didn't give up on God's help, and I knew He'd never give up on me.

1966: Guardian Angel School, Wisconsin

One of our parish priests, Father John, who was a concert pianist, was endeavoring to form an adult choir in church. He asked that another young man and I perform a duet for a special feast day Mass. I was delighted for this opportunity to praise God with my song. However, Sister Mary Elizabeth, our superior and principal, squelched the idea because I wasn't supposed to perform anywhere without permission—and she wouldn't provide the permission. What a disappointment!

There was no piano in the rectory, so Father John frequently came over to the convent to practice on ours. It was located in a very large room on the lower level of our building. I loved hearing him play, so I often sat in the back of the room to listen to his piano and voice concert.

One afternoon, Father John asked me to sing along with him; we had a great time. He knew I loved to sing, but since I had no formal training, he offered to give me private singing lessons. I was delighted! However, I couldn't get the permission for this opportunity. I was told I had no need of voice lessons because I was a classroom teacher, not a musician. Sister Mary Elizabeth also said I was becoming too friendly with Father John, so I could no longer be in the room with him while he practiced. When he was apprised of this situation, he seldom practiced at the convent anymore.

We had fifteen Sisters in our convent. A woman was hired to cook our lunch and dinner, but she refused to make our breakfast because it was too early for her. Thus, the younger Sisters took turns preparing that meal. Because of our schedule for morning prayers, we had a limited time to prepare breakfast; we organized as much as we could the night before.

We often laid out trays of bacon so they were ready to be placed in the oven in the morning. However, it was imperative to cover these trays very tightly because this was an old building, and mice ran rampant near the kitchen. They not only scooted around the floor, they also enjoyed eating our raw bacon. I was frightened when I saw these creatures, and if they came near me, I would jump on a chair and scream, even during Profound Silence.

Our parishioners were very active in all the church and school activities. One evening, the Boy Scouts' den mother called to ask if one of us would put a sign on the church door, indicating there would be no meeting that evening. She expressed her regrets, but she had no babysitter. Without even thinking, I volunteered to babysit her children. She was delighted, so she quickly picked me up and brought me to her home. I knew her children well, so we had a good time while their mom was at her meeting,

The next morning, I was in big trouble because I went out in the evening without permission, and I offered my services to babysit. I was appalled at Sister Mary Elizabeth's next comment: "Where is the money you received for babysitting?" Of course there was none! It seemed as if I couldn't do anything to please her.

I was invited to stay at one of the other convents for a weekend. The building was cold, so besides our electric blankets, each bedroom had a small electric heater. In my haste to get to morning prayers and Mass on time, I forgot to turn off the heater, and I must have accidentally kicked it under the bed. When I left the room, I closed the door.

We had a delicious lunch, and we played board games all afternoon. When it was time to leave, I went to the bedroom to collect my suitcase and personal belongings. As soon as I opened the door, spontaneous combustion occurred, and the mattress burst into flames.

By the time the fire department arrived, the drapes and a chair were inflamed, too. The firemen threw the mattress, drapes, and chair out the window, but everything else in the room was completely charred. (Unfortunately, the nuns at that convent had to endure the smell of smoke for many weeks.)

One of their parish priests saw the fire engines in front of the convent, so he ran over to see what was happening. When I told him I caused the fire, I was crying. He spoke to me very gently. He said the parish would handle everything through insurance, and the burned items would be replaced. He was very kind, but I was inconsolable.

I was embarrassed to return to my convent and leave all the devastation behind me, but I was supposed to be home by five o'clock. However, when I returned to my convent, I realized my clothes reeked from smoke, so I ran upstairs to change them. I threw all my smoke-filled clothes down our clothes chute without thinking they actually stank, and they would contaminate the other clothing in the chute.

The next morning, Sister Mary Elizabeth and two other Sisters sniffed smoke. They were walking all around the convent, trying to find its source. Of course, it was from the clothes I had sent down the chute. When I saw their anxiety, I confessed to what happened the previous day. None of the Sisters could believe I had been so careless. My superior never let me live it down. At our conferences, she brought it up over and over.

While feelings were still raw about the fire I caused, it was imperative for me to have both my big toenails removed surgically because they were seriously infected. After the operation I was unable to walk down the stairs, but Sister Mary Elizabeth said it was a shame that I expected the older Sisters to bring meal trays to a young nun like me. I was humiliated, so I made every effort to stagger downstairs as soon as possible. I even went back to school before the doctor released me.

I missed three days of school. When the children saw me on the playground, they ran to tell me they missed me. That made me feel great because I knew *they* cared. They were more empathetic than my superior.

About that time, there was a break-in at the convent. Without saying anything to us, Sister Mary Elizabeth purchased a huge police dog named Roger. I have an inordinate fear of animals, particularly large dogs, so I was terrified when I saw the animal. We had two stairwells, one at each end of the hall. I used the one farthest from the dog and ran to my bedroom. I wasn't willing to go downstairs for dinner, but Sister Mary Elizabeth sent one of the nuns upstairs to get me.

I tried to stay away from Roger as much as possible, but sometimes he roamed the convent halls. When I saw him, I fled to the first safe area I could find. I actually lived in terror.

I was disgusted to see that, instead of purchasing special dishes for Roger, the nuns let him use *our* dishes. Then they washed these dishes along with the ones we used. When I complained, I was told that "dogs are cleaner than people."

Roger was always brought to our community room where we recreated. Fortunately, it was a long room, so I stayed at the opposite end, away from where the dog was playing. When Roger was trained, the word **attack** was used to tell him to confront an intruder. Therefore, we were told to never use that word around him. Even after we'd been directed not to say that word, one of our older Sisters wanted to see what would happen when Roger was riled up. She'd say things like, "I hope I will never have a heart *attack*" or "It was fun to see the *attack* during the football game." When she did that, I fled from the room.

Apparently, Roger had also been trained with long poles. On a patriotic holiday, I was putting our flag in its holder. The dog saw the long pole and came running after me. I threw down the pole and flag and ran from the room.

When I learned I was being transferred again, I thanked God! This was one mission I was happy to leave.

12

Chapter

SUMMERS: 1966 AND 1967

Sisters' Summer Orchestra

When I was in high school, I was a trombonist. Upon my return to the motherhouse one summer, I was invited to join an orchestra comprised of nuns who were music teachers. They needed a trombonist.

Sister Mary Cecile directed our high school band and orchestra, and she also directed the Sisters' summer orchestra. Since she knew I played the trombone, she asked Sister Mary Roselyn, my summer superior, if I could be part of this semiprofessional ensemble. Sister Mary Roselyn was reluctant to agree with this plan because, it was noted once again, that I wasn't a music teacher. She saw no reason for me to be making music when I should be working toward my degree. However, Sister Mary Cecile was quite persuasive, so I eventually joined this impressive group of musicians.

One afternoon, I was practicing my music in the conservatory. It was a huge edifice, but since it was practically empty for the summer, my practice resounded throughout the building. I kept playing one section of my sonata over and over again until I was sure I had it right. All at once, one of the conservatory directors came into my practice room saying, "You need to play an A# in that spot. You're driving me crazy with that wrong note!" I was truly deflated!

Summer Classes

When I returned to the motherhouse the following summer, I took a history class taught by Sister Augusta, one of my favorite former superiors. I had always been a B or C student, so when she gave us a quick quiz and I received 80 percent, she called me aside to ask what happened. I told her this was a common grade for me. She replied, "I won't accept grades like this from you. You are smart, and grades of this caliber are unacceptable".

She asked to see my notes. They were beautifully typed and placed neatly in my notebook. Then she asked me what I'd done with them. I responded that I'd read them several times. She declared, "You don't know how to study!"

She sat down with me, and we went over every paragraph in the chapter, highlighting the main sentence of each one. When we finished, we made an outline and then reviewed what I had learned. From that time on, I used this technique for all my classes. Although this is the way most students study, this process was new to me. Due to Sister Augusta's assistance, and her confidence in me, I became an A student in most classes, including those in my graduate studies.

Death of My Dad

One morning when we were in church for our morning prayers, Reverend Mother came down the aisle, touched my shoulder, and indicated that I should follow her out of the church. When we reached the hallway, she told me my father died that morning. She said arrangements were being made for me to be with my mother in Chicago.

I went upstairs, packed a few things, and returned to Reverend Mother's office. She gave me train tickets, and one of the workmen drove me to the station. But there was a problem! I was told it was imperative that I stay in a convent. Although there was a Dominican convent right across the street from my parents' home, the nuns had closed it for the summer; they were taking classes at their own motherhouse in Indiana. I asked if I could stay with my mom, but this request was denied.

Father Conners, the pastor, called the Dominican motherhouse and told them he needed at least two nuns to return to the convent so I could stay there. I was embarrassed that so much inconvenience was caused by our outdated rules, especially when my mother lived so close by.

When my dad died, he was in one hospital and my mother was in another one on the verge of a nervous breakdown. It had been difficult for her to take care of Dad for so many years. When he was well, Dad had a delightful, outgoing personality. However, all that changed after his third stroke. He spoke to my mother in a demeaning manner. He said she was poisoning his food, and when she was bathing him, he told her she was hurting him on purpose. She spent a lot of time crying, and things finally caught up with her.

Father Conners knew that Mom had been away for some time, so he realized she probably didn't have much food in the house. He brought me over to the rectory, and he went through his deepfreeze and pantry; he gave me three large bags of food to bring home. I told him his cook might be upset when so much food was missing. He said, "She's used to that."

Father Conners was often considered to be eccentric, but he was always kind to those in need. He was extremely considerate to us throughout our period of grief. I was very grateful to him for his sympathy and generosity.

At that time, wakes were held for three days. My two sisters and I greeted the guests as they entered the funeral home, but in many cases, none of us knew these family friends. When the visitors arrived, we looked at each other to see if any of us recognized them; we usually came up empty-handed. Because we had taken Mom from the hospital so she could attend the wake, she was still on strong medication; she didn't recognize some of her friends either.

I was grateful for the permission to attend Dad's wake, but I was required to leave the funeral home by six o'clock in the evening. When workpeople came a little later to console my family, they were disappointed that I wasn't there. The funeral home closed at nine o'clock p.m. I was frustrated to know my mother was home alone while I was in such close proximity— right across the street.

When I returned to our motherhouse after the funeral, I resumed my classes and made up the work I'd missed. However, it was difficult to concentrate on schoolwork when I was concerned that my mother wasn't snapping out of her depression. Within a month after my dad's death, she decided to sell the house and move to Florida, where my sister Colleen lived.

When Mom was packing up the house, I was permitted to help her. She picked me up after school in her little VW, and although she still drove erratically, she managed to get us from the convent to her home and back again. (It didn't help that Mom was still on heavy medication.) It was hard for my mom to concentrate on everything that needed to be done in the house. Each evening, when I went home, I left some things for her to pack. When I returned the next day, most of these things were still where I left them. Mom stood near the boxes and just stared at them. Things were too overwhelming for her.

Eventually, everything Mom wanted to keep was packed. She gave her furniture and all her other household furnishings to the parish thrift store in the inner city. Although I wouldn't have been allowed to keep anything from the house, I often wonder how many of her furnishings would have good value today.

13

Chapter

❦

MISSIONS: 1967–1968

1967: St. Martin de Porres School, Illinois

I loved this assignment in the inner city. Although the families were poor, they always managed to pay their tuition at our Catholic school so their children could obtain a better education. Since these parents sacrificed so much for their children, we had total cooperation from them.

There were sixty-two youngsters in my sixth-grade class. James was always cooperative, and he usually followed the rules very well. However, one day he kept talking to his friends who sat around him. Because he was ordinarily so good, I didn't want to scold him, so I told him to sit in the back of the room where I couldn't see him. His older brother heard about this incident and reported it to their mother.

Every morning when the school bell rang, the children lined up quietly to enter the building. James was slightly out of line, so I touched him on the shoulder to remind him to stay in a straight line. He cringed and glared at me. This was so unusual for him that I asked him what was wrong. At first he ignored me, but he finally admitted that his mother had *"wupped"* him for talking in school. I pulled back his shirt, and when I saw what she had done to him, I was appalled. She had *scourged* him with an ironing cord.

I called James's mother and asked why she had punished him so severely. She said that if her boys were in trouble at school, they would be in more trouble at home. I told her I appreciated her cooperation, but this punishment was excessive. Although she didn't agree with me, she conceded that she'd try not to become so angry with the boys that she hurt them.

In order to keep these youngsters off the streets after school, I became their basketball coach. Although we didn't win a championship, we still won lots of games. We were all proud of this achievement.

When the basketball season ended, I formed a glee club. This was a group of fifth- and sixth-graders who were interested in joining a choral group and learning some folk dances. Almost everyone from these classes participated in this activity. They couldn't wait to get started. We met after school three days each week. They were all very proud to be a part of this group; there were no discipline problems.

The children were quite excited when they heard a radio announcement stating that the Navy Glee Club would perform on a particular date. They thought this message was about *our* glee club because they were under the impression we were the only glee club around.

Our glee club prepared a program of songs and folk dances for an evening performance in our school auditorium. Parents, aunts, uncles, grandparents, and neighbors crowded the hall. No one expected the performance to be so delightful. The children were very proud of themselves, as well they should have been. Some of the parents thought we should have charged an admission fee, but of course, that's something I would never consider in that part of the city.

After the program, several mothers were waiting for me near the auditorium door. They handed me an envelope that contained $100. They said this gift was an expression of their gratitude for all I was doing for their children. I was really *touched!* Despite the fact they had so little themselves, they presented this generous gift to me with great love.

At times, some of the mothers invited me to their homes for a little afternoon visit. I was honored by these invitations because our people needed to trust someone before allowing that person to enter their home.

At John's home, his mother offered me a glass of lemonade. As I was enjoying this refreshment, John came into the kitchen with his lemonade in a jar. I said, "Oh, you get to drink yours out of a jar."

He responded, "Yeah, you have our glass!"

My stomach lurched! These families lived in dire poverty, and yet they were willing to share what little they had. Once again I realized I had taken a vow of poverty, but these people *lived* poverty every day.

We were loved by the people in our neighborhood. I always felt safe because I knew they would protect me. However, I did have one bad experience. The nearby high school was having a talent show, and I was scheduled to sing. When I was walking there, a man confronted me and dragged me into the alley. There were always lots of police around that neighborhood so I calmly said, "You see all those police over there? Let me go or I'll scream!"

He said, "Oh, it's like that? Okay." And he let me go. Although I was shaken, I was all right. I didn't tell the nuns about this experience because I knew they would be upset and fearful. However, I'm not sure how it happened, but some of our neighbors heard about this incident. They apologized to me profusely. I knew this was an isolated incident, but they figured that someone should have been around to protect me.

It was a sad day when Martin Luther King was killed. Our school was right there, only a mile from where the riots started. We sent the children home from school where they would be safer. As the riots came closer to us, there was a great deal of looting, breaking of store windows, and setting fire to buildings—so many good people were being affected.

My mother was watching TV in Florida. When she saw the fire engines and all the destruction getting close to our convent, she called to see if I was all right. I assured her I was fine, but she still worried about me. Later, she called again. She was even more concerned when she was told I wasn't home; I had gone to assist our friends and neighbors.

All the nuns knew the neighborhood residents; most of those who were destroying the community were outsiders. However, when some parents saw on TV that their own children were participating in the looting, they were devastated. None of the loot was ever allowed in their homes.

While the nuns were following this terrible episode on TV, three of us went up to the convent roof where we saw these disgusting intruders running with plastic bags from the neighborhood dry-cleaners.

Because some of our parish children lived upstairs from the store, all three of us ran over there. Two nuns stayed downstairs to see if they could make any sense of the destruction taking place; I went upstairs to ensure the family was safe. Fortunately, they had gone elsewhere for protection.

I was horrified at what I saw. Some of these thugs were removing food from the refrigerator and pitching it against the wall. Others found tablecloths and other linens in a drawer; they were ripping them apart. Everything else in the apartment was scattered on the floor. I saw someone throw a lamp on the floor and stomp on it.

I tried to gather framed pictures and other items I presumed would be meaningful to the family. However, every time I made a pile of things to take with me, when I turned around, the stack was gone. This was *very* disheartening! I finally picked up a few items and went downstairs to see how the other Sisters were faring. They thought I had gone home, so they went back to the convent without me.

That's when I saw two huge men carrying the cash register. Even though it was probably empty, I thought, "They'd even take the family's last money." I actually pushed one of these men, demanding they put the cashbox down. They glared at me, used some expletives, and told me to "get lost." Then they tripped on clothes that were scattered on the ground, so they had to set it down.

I immediately sat on the cash register, folded my arms, and glared at them. Both men were extremely angry. One of them pulled out a knife and threatened to use it on me. The other man said, "Be careful … that's a nun!" After some more foul language, they spit at me and left. Throughout this ordeal, I was never afraid of being hurt. I was simply outraged!

On my way back to the convent, I saw people being thrown out of cars and others fighting with each other. There was a lot of screaming. People were calling obscenities to those in cars, and rocks were being thrown indiscriminately. As I hurried along I felt as though I was participating in a bad dream.

As soon as I arrived back at the convent and closed the

door, my whole body started shaking. Everything I had seen flashed before me. I was overwhelmed! I couldn't even discuss this terrible experience when the other Sisters questioned me about it.

That evening, several of us returned to our roof. We saw the devastation surrounding us; the demolition of the neighborhood was unbelievable. When the dry-cleaners burned to the ground, I was relieved, because it meant the family would never see the destruction of their home and place of business.

Many parishes immediately collected food and sent it to us; it was stored in our auditorium. Father Kubis, the pastor, slept there to protect the food; he knew that hungry, desperate people might break in and steal it. Many people now had no place to go for shelter or food because their homes were destroyed, and most of their stores were damaged or burned.

The following day, when it was announced we had food available, streams of people came to get it. Father told me to organize the volunteers. We were to give the people whatever they asked for. No matter how much they said they needed, we were to provide them with the food they requested.

We told Father we saw people selling the food down at the corner. He replied, "When Jesus gave a gift, He didn't stipulate how it was to be used." We were very tired, but somehow we found the energy to keep going. Father was our inspiration. He worked tirelessly.

Later, we all went through the neighborhood to help people plow through the rubble of their homes—seeking a picture frame or perhaps a coin or medal. What a heartbreaking scene!

The inner city was a place I loved. I hoped I would be left there forever, but I was transferred again. Why? It probably had something to do with me helping Father Kubis build community. It was frowned upon that I assisted him with his parish projects. What a pity! I loved the people, and they loved and trusted me. Yet I was being taken away from them.

I knew it was time for me to speak up. I went to my superior and asked why I couldn't stay there since so few Sisters wanted to work in the inner city. She abruptly said, "You shouldn't question the Will of God."

Father Kubis was livid with the superior's response to me, so he approached her and requested that I stay in the parish. She was adamant. She said, "God has spoken so there will be no change in Sister Mary's transfer." Father Kubis was very angry, and I was resentful.

Times like this were one of the reasons I eventually severed my relations with my Community. I could no longer accept that these transfers were being done in my best interests. Again, what really were my best interests? What did that mean? Rebellion reigned in my heart. Even though I didn't stay silent, my faith in God began to waver. I asked God if He was abandoning me.

1968: Peace and Unity School, Indiana

This school was located in a lower-income area. I missed the inner city dreadfully, but I could relate well to the people of this town. Because of its location, it was difficult to hire teachers for our school. We were fortunate to have some very good teachers, but sometimes we kept those who were mediocre because we had no one to replace them.

I was assigned to fourth grade *and* sixth grade. While I was teaching fourth grade in the morning, Miss Kahn taught sixth grade in her classroom. However, she couldn't control these youngsters, so we exchanged classes in the afternoon. As I came down the hall leading to her classroom, I could hear the noise emanating from her room. I always took a deep breath and prayed for God's help when entering this turbulent situation.

Even though only a few youngsters tried to listen to what I said, I made a great effort to teach this class to respect others and to try being good leaders in their classroom. We spent a lot of time picking up papers and spitballs they had fired at one another; we also cleaned out desks stuffed with incomplete assignments. Most of the students were more interested in playing with one another than they were in cooperating with me. They were totally out of control! I was exhausted when I left them. The other Sisters in the convent were sympathetic; from time to time, they offered to take one of the unruly sixth-grade leaders to their classrooms. I always appreciated that gesture.

Meanwhile, Miss Kahn was supposed to be teaching my fourth-grade class. Unfortunately, that didn't work well, either. The children were permitted to walk around the room, and they were allowed to talk with their friends, play blackboard games, or draw pictures if they finished their assignments. Of course, they did their work in a slipshod manner so they could spend their time drawing and playing. Each morning, when I returned to my fourth-grade classroom, I required the children to redo most of their assigned papers and clean up the mess left over from the previous afternoon.

Working in this school was a difficult experience, but when I was transferred again, I couldn't believe it. The very idea that I wasn't needed there made me feel insignificant. When I was alone, I cried bitterly. However, I no longer wanted to carry the burden of anger, so I asked God to gift me with peace of heart.

14
Chapter

EDUCATION: M.ED.

1964–1968: Marion University, Minnesota (Summers)

It was my privilege to begin my studies for a Masters Degree in Education at Marion University. I loved every minute of my program. My living quarters were the best! Our building was new, and it was air-conditioned. Two of us shared a suite that had two separate bedrooms; between the bedrooms was a large study area where two long desks with fluorescent lighting were provided. These arrangements couldn't have been any better.

During my first year at the university, the faculty was exploring a new curriculum technique. Only one class at a time could be selected. This course lasted four hours each day for two weeks. Semester exams were given at the end of the first week, and final exams took place at the end of the second week. Part of the final exam was to present a comprehensive paper to the professor.

Most of the summer students were nuns. The few laypeople who attended classes had family responsibilities, along with their studies. For them, the new curriculum was not conducive to their family needs. I was so fortunate that my only responsibility was to handle my classes conscientiously.

I responded well to this curriculum. I had to think about only one subject, and I could devote all my time to it. Because of Sister Augusta's assistance in teaching me how to study, I received an A or an A+ in every class.

Although this curriculum was successful for most courses, the faculty realized that subjects like philosophy, economics, and European history needed more time. The following year, those classes were modified to a three-week pattern.

When I received my M.Ed. degree, I was elated! I will always be grateful to my Community for providing me the opportunity to obtain this degree, especially at an outstanding institution.

15
Chapter

MOM'S NEW LIFESTYLE

When Mom sold her home in Chicago, she purchased a mobile home in Florida. She was very happy in her new surroundings. Her health was better, she enjoyed the weather, and she had good neighbors. However, after about two years, Bill, her next door neighbor, told her that a senior residence was being built by the Archdiocese of Florida; he said he intended to move there. My mom went to view the layout, and she decided to join him.

Without telling Colleen, Mom made all the arrangements to relocate. However, this new building was located thirty miles from where my sister lived. Before Mom moved to the senior residence, Colleen could easily schedule time to take her to her doctors or pick up a few things for her after work. Now, the distance made my mom's needs more prohibitive. .

When Colleen called me about this situation, I sympathized with her, but I said I couldn't be much help to her since I lived so far away. In my mind, I knew Mom would be in good hands with Colleen. She was always the one to handle big matters. I could have called her from time to time to give her some support. Sad to say, I'd learned to detach myself from family issues, so my phone calls to her were few and far between.

Mom's new building had several means of contacting personnel in case of an emergency. One way was for the residents to pull a long cord located in the bathroom. However, my mother didn't like that cord hanging there, so she tied it up high. She also had a buzzer near her bed. For some reason, she hung a picture over it. Another security measure was for each resident to turn a key upright in an assigned mailbox in the morning. This alerted the staff to know whether or not everyone was up and about. Bill didn't sleep well, so during the night he walked around the building. He turned Mom's key in her mailbox so she wouldn't need to come downstairs in the morning.

One morning, while Mom was making her bed, she fell and broke her hip. Since she had tried to beat the system, she had no way of contacting anyone. She lay on the floor for several hours until the staff noticed she'd missed lunch.

Colleen called to let me know what happened, but once again, I was of no help to her. I knew she was handling things, as usual, so I seldom called to give her any support. Even at times like this, I couldn't comprehend her need.

While my mom was in the hospital, she went into a deep depression. She refused to get out of her wheelchair, and she rejected most of her food. She was moved to the psychiatric ward to see if she would respond any better. She made no progress there either. Her psychiatrist wanted to give her shock treatments, but Mom refused them.

The psychiatrist called Colleen and sent to Chicago for me. He said Mom was going deeper and deeper into her depression, and without shock treatments, he didn't think she would survive mentally. Although today's laws would never allow this, Colleen and I both agreed that he should go ahead with the shock treatments on the following Monday.

On Sunday, Colleen went to my mother's hospital room and started hanging up clothes she had washed. My mom said very curtly, "It's about time you got here!" Colleen was very tired, and Mom had "touched a nerve." Colleen became so angry that she started yelling at Mom, which was something we *never* did! Mom was so disturbed by Colleen's conduct that she actually stood up from her wheelchair and started shouting at my sister. It didn't take long before the nurses ran into the room and sent my sister home.

Colleen was distraught! She called to tell me what happened. I finally started to realize she was under a huge strain. The good news was: as soon as Colleen finished talking with me, the psychiatrist called her and said she'd given Mom the shock she needed. There would be no shock treatment the next day.

Mom started recuperating, and she was soon ready to be discharged. That brought up another issue: her doctor thought she shouldn't live alone anymore. Once again, it was up to Colleen to handle the situation. She called me, looking for support, but I could only commiserate with her. As I look back on this situation, I can't believe how thoughtless I was.

There really wasn't much choice for Mom's housing. Colleen said she could live with her *unless* Mom started complaining about the children or criticizing her for things beyond her control.

With Mom in the house, Colleen's stress was increased. She had four children who needed attention. She was trying to help them with their homework, do her job as a salesperson, cook the meals, and clean the house. The children helped where they could, but like other children, they were eager to get outside to play.

At times, Colleen felt overwhelmed. To relax, she did exquisite needlepoint projects. I am fortunate to have several of them in my home.

Mom watched *Perry Mason* every afternoon. When Joe came home from school, he wanted to see a science program, so he just changed the channel. Mom didn't complain because she didn't want Colleen to make her leave. It took a little time, but my sister finally realized what was going on. She handled the situation promptly.

In those days, parents knew their children were safe when they were outside. The only rule was: "Be home before dark."

James and Joe spent their time, among other things, swimming in the creek, fishing, riding their bikes, exploring abandoned buildings, and hanging on the backs of trucks while they were in motion. They both enjoyed planning science experiments, and they were proud to exhibit some of them at school. After they graduated from high school, they separately enlisted in the Navy. As it happened, they were each deployed overseas where they saw "war at its worst." This changed their lives forever. When they left the Navy, Joe became a registered nurse, and James became a certified automotive technician.

Danielle liked to play cards and board games with her brothers; she followed them around every chance she got. In her teen years, she took small jobs so she'd have money to hang out with her friends at the mall. When Danielle married, she had four children who have all been very successful in their adult careers.

Jack, Colleen's oldest son, was interested in photography, electronics, and his treasured guitar. He spent many hours writing new instrumental music for a band he formed. He also photographed wild life and their habitats. When he enlisted in the Army, he was deployed as a photographer in areas of devastating combat. This experience affected his whole life. He turned to music for comfort.

After he left the Army, he married and had one son who followed in his father's footsteps by becoming a professional guitarist.

16
Chapter

FAMILY EVENTS

Vacations with Colleen

Because I had completed my M.Ed., I was allowed to take vacations with my sister. Colleen enjoyed cruises to the Caribbean, but she didn't like to travel alone, so she paid for me to come along with her. What a privilege!

Colleen and I enjoyed each other, and our trips were incredible. Besides the picturesque islands, we saw a way of life where many islanders were anxious to show us their artistry and places of interest. Other islanders dejectedly pointed to their homes where they lived in dire poverty.

Before we reached each island, the activities director from the ship met with us to explain traits of the island we were approaching: what to purchase and not to purchase; not to take pictures of the people without asking their permission; and if we started giving quarters to some children, we would soon have a flock of more children surrounding us. The director said not to believe the islanders when they said their wooden artwork was made from mahogany. She told us to run our fingernail down the item, and we'd find that most carvings had been colored with shoe polish. Nevertheless, some were so intricate that we bought them an anyway.

The natives expected us to barter with them. I've never been good at that, but I soon learned it was important to do so. I wanted to purchase a particular wood carving, but the price was more than I wanted to pay. The artist asked me what I thought was a fair price. When I told him, he put his head in his hands and claimed I was cheating him. I felt guilty and decided not to purchase the item after all. However, when our bus was leaving, he ran beside it and said I could have it for the price I suggested.

Colleen and I took several cruises. While we were on board each ship, there was always an announcement that all the friends of Bill Wilson should meet in a particular room at a certain time. I thought Bill Wilson must be a very wealthy man to travel on so many ships and have a special room assigned to him for his business meetings. I learned later that Bill Wilson was one of the founders of Alcoholics Anonymous, and these announcements were for scheduled AA meetings.

Death of My Mom

In 1970, shortly after my last cruise with Colleen, our mother died. She often talked about death. She said when she died, she wanted a three-day wake in Florida and another three-day wake in Chicago, because that's where her cemetery plot was located. However, when she moved to her senior apartment, she had only a few remaining acquaintances; she had lost contact with all her Chicago friends, and she had isolated herself from most of her Floridian friends.

We ended up having a *three-hour* wake near her apartment

building on a Sunday afternoon. A few people from her building came to pay their respects.

Colleen no longer attended Mass, but she was always willing to bring me to church and pick me up later. The Sunday we were having my mother's wake, Colleen asked me to leave the church immediately after Mass because she still had some arrangements to take care of at the funeral home.

As soon as Mass was over, and the last hymn was being played, I got up to leave. However, when I reached the exit, a huge man was blocking my way. I said I needed to leave, but he stretched his arms across the doorway and stared straight ahead; he wouldn't budge. I tried another exit at the side of the church, only to meet with the same bullying. To remind the parishioners not to leave early, there was a sign at the door that read, "Judas left early, too."

When I was finally released from the church, I went to the pastor who was speaking with someone in front of the church. I butted into his conversation and told him what I thought about forcing people to remain in church. He asked me why I wanted to leave early, so I told him I was going to my mother's funeral. He had no sympathy, indicating it was not acceptable to leave the church early under any circumstance.

Colleen was waiting impatiently in the car. She wanted to know what that was all about. I said I'd tell her later because I was actually too angry to talk about it at the time. I knew if I told her what really happened, she would be livid. She was under a lot of stress, and I didn't want to give her any more fodder.

Since my mom already had a cemetery plot in Chicago, the funeral director in Florida shipped her body to Chicago. At the cemetery, we had a simple graveside service for her. Jeanette, Ed, and the children all attended this early morning ceremony. Afterward, we all went to a nearby restaurant where we were able to express our feelings of loss.

17

Chapter

COMMUNITY INVOLVEMENT

1969: St Francis Assisi School, Wisconsin

Pope John Paul directed religious Communities to become more involved with people in need. In response to the pope's encyclical (a document called *Vatican II*), five Sisters, including myself, petitioned our higher superiors to allow us to work in other capacities, along with our classroom responsibilities. We were granted this permission, with the understanding it was an *experiment*, and the approval could be withdrawn at any time.

All five of us were transferred to one convent where we set about making new clothes, finding ways to fix our hair, and using makeup. It was an exciting time for us. We felt like founders of a new way of life.

Many Sisters in the Community were very much against this experiment, and they were quite vocal in their dissent. They claimed we would all leave the Community in a very short time.

(Actually, within two years, three of our five Sisters *did* leave. My departure was several years later.)

We were no longer using our religious names, so we reverted back to our given names. This was a totally different lifestyle; I related well to this more leisurely way of life. We had no superior; each of us was equal. This was a responsibility I cherished.

I could now dedicate my life to God more fully. I truly felt God's love for me, and I began to reclaim my self-esteem. The lack of rigidity was good for me. No blind obedience!

Although we were still teaching in the school, we also became involved with diverse community activities, so some of our schedules differed. There was no regular routine, and it was up to each of us to live our lives as we thought we were Called. We were quite unassuming, and we had very simple rules.

Because we were so close to one another, I was deeply hurt when the other four sisters went somewhere on my birthday, and they didn't return until late that evening. I saw them leave, but I presumed they were going out to purchase a birthday cake for me.

We always had a festive meal for special days, but since nobody notified our cook about my birthday, she prepared leftovers for the meal. I was so disappointed! I could hardly touch the food because I was so upset about eating this type of meal all by myself—on my birthday. I went to bed crying and feeling sorry for myself.

The next morning, I confronted two Sisters and said sarcastically, "Thanks for making my birthday so memorable." One Sister responded by saying, "You're welcome."

I was stunned! This was the first rift in our little group. I never did find out where they went or why they were so nasty.

Almost every evening, our pastor, Father George, came to the convent to chat with us. Sometimes he stayed late, so most of us excused ourselves early to get ready for bed. Sister Lorraine always stayed with him, supposedly because she didn't think it was proper to ask him to leave.

After a few months, Sister Lorraine came to my classroom saying, "I came to say good-bye." I asked her where she was going. She said she and Father George were leaving; they were going to get married. I couldn't believe my ears! Sister Lorraine was leaving her Community, and Father George was leaving his priesthood. I felt sick to my stomach. Never did I imagine that Father's late nights at our convent were really dates with Sister Lorraine.

About a month after Sister Lorraine's departure, Sisters Mary Ann and Diane told me they were both leaving, too. They didn't explain where they were going or what they would be doing, but at that point I was so devastated, I didn't care. It seemed that the concerns of our Sisters, who had expressed doubt about our experiment, were coming true.

Since Sister Josephine and I were the only ones left, our superiors said the convent building was too big for us. They found a lovely house in a pleasant neighborhood where we would be living *among the people*. We had to travel a bit to school, but under the circumstances, that wasn't too difficult.

Our neighbors were wonderful; they frequently brought casseroles and desserts to us. Sometimes they stayed to visit. Although some of them weren't Catholic, they respected us and offered to do anything they could to make our lives easier. Sometimes they even drove us to school.

One evening, our next-door neighbors came over to invite us to a neighborhood meeting. This was an opportunity for us to participate in a community event, so we accepted the invitation wholeheartedly. While we were chatting, I saw a trail of six mice meandering to my bedroom. I still can't believe it, but I actually controlled myself and didn't mention the mice while our visitors were there. However, I became absolutely irrational when they left.

Sister Josephine and I searched everywhere in my bedroom— under the bed, on the bed, under my sheets, on the windowsill, in my cabinet drawers—but there was no sign of the mice. I stayed in another bedroom that night, but I didn't sleep a wink.

Sister Mary Lois, who was the superior for nuns who didn't reside in a convent, came to our house to meet with Sister Josephine and me. She said we would be returning to a convent the next year. We would be wearing our modified Habits, and we would resume traditional Community living.

Since I'd experienced a taste of a more relaxed lifestyle, I was distressed about this decision. Living among the people and working within their neighborhood allowed me to live the way Pope John XXIII requested. I really didn't want to go back to a rigid lifestyle. I prayed that God would work one of His miracles for me.

1970–1980: Apartment Living, Illinois

God *did* answer my prayer the way I hoped. Sister Maria was living in an apartment by herself because her previous companion preferred to return to Community life. The superiors didn't want Sister Maria to live alone, so they sent me to live with her. Of course, I was delighted.

Sister Maria was an all-around artist. She was involved in many community activities, especially with our parish church as well as with another Christian church. Our parish was more conservative, so she couldn't' plan too many activities, for them, but at the Christian church she provided unique services with dancing, singing, miming, painting, and more.

What a delightful person! We got along well. I enjoyed hearing about her projects, and she was interested in everything I did. She was always supportive when I needed special friendship.

Maria usually had meetings, and I was teaching in a private school. We went our separate ways each morning, but we were usually home in the early evening so we could have dinner together. If one of us needed to rest rather than eat, that was fine. If one of us needed to be at an evening meeting, the other one gladly washed the dishes. Sister Maria was noted in the neighborhood community for all the joy she spread. All in all, I couldn't have been happier.

18
Chapter

BUSINESS WORLD: 1972–1976

Our Community was educationally based, and most nuns were classroom teachers. I didn't think I could face another classroom experience, so I asked permission to take a job outside the Community parameters. After much discussion and many meetings with Reverend Mother and higher superiors, I was reluctantly allowed to do this *temporarily*, with the stipulation this position would be something in the field of education.

As I embraced my new lifestyle, I asked God to direct me and help me do the best job possible. It was no secret that I was a nun, so in my mind, that meant people would have higher expectations of me. For a while, I reverted to trying to be the person others expected me to be. Eventually I realized, once again, that I didn't need to spend my time trying to please others; instead, I asked daily for God's guidance to be the person He wanted me to be.

1972–1976: Private Tutoring School

I became a teacher at a private tutoring school. It was a pleasure to teach students one-on-one! Most of them came from wealthy homes. Some came because they didn't want to attend a regular school; others came for assistance with subjects that were difficult for them in school.

David lived in the inner city. He came to our school on a government grant. When he enrolled, he was reading on a first-grade level. He improved to the point where he passed the Illinois State Board of Education's eighth-grade examination. Everyone was excited for him. We had a party at school, and I decided to take him to a nice restaurant for lunch.

That was a big mistake! David had never been in an upscale restaurant, so he felt out of place. He was embarrassed when he was handed a menu because he didn't know its purpose. I suggested that he might like a hamburger, and he agreed. When we were leaving, I left a tip on the table. I was up front paying the bill when he came rushing up to me with the money because he thought I had accidentally left it there. David would have been much more comfortable if I had taken him to McDonald's.

David kept progressing with his studies, and he proudly wore his backpack with all his schoolbooks. However, one day when he was on his way to school, he was confronted by some gang members. Shockingly, they shot him in the head and killed him. We were all devastated. What a tragedy!

Meanwhile, the school's director of education resigned, and I was given her position. I hired teachers, planned their schedules, audited their classes, and edited proposals for Mr. English, the owner of the school. When teachers didn't appear for their classes, I tried to find substitutes, but most of the time I taught the classes myself. Since they earned only four dollars per hour with no benefits, most of the teachers weren't too dedicated.

When the teachers' checks started bouncing, Mr. English always had an excuse: he had written the checks on the wrong account, or there was a bank error, or he forgot to sign them. He replaced the bad checks, but one time he replaced their bad checks with other bad checks. The teachers were really disgruntled. They left the school as soon as they procured another job. A large part of my day was dedicated to interviewing and hiring teachers.

Mr. English gave me many time-consuming projects to complete. Some of them took an inordinate amount of time. I even worked on them at home, but when I finished the projects, he just left them on his desk. When I asked him why he wasn't using them, his response was, "I'm keeping them for later."

He told me to continue providing information for other projects. I found this directive to be very disconcerting because I surmised that, just like all the other assignments, he wouldn't use them in any capacity. However, I did as I was told. (This was just like blind obedience in the convent.)

Our school was located in a new high-rise building in a congested area of downtown Chicago. Furriers, accountants, jewelers, and cosmetic firms were situated on the same floor as our school. There were general bathrooms in the hall that both the businesspeople and our students used. We often received compliments about how well our pupils behaved. Mr. English was proud of our reputation, so he appreciated these comments from the businesspeople.

Mr. English was very chauvinistic. At that time, most women wore dresses or suits to work, and he often mentioned how professional they looked. However, when one female teacher appeared in a pantsuit, I was told to send out a memo indicating that pantsuits were not appropriate apparel for our school, and all women were to continue wearing dresses. I said I couldn't do that, because I personally thought pantsuits were more modest than the miniskirts that were in vogue. Some of our younger teachers wore these short dresses, and when they bent over, our male students were delighted to view their exposed lingerie.

Despite my resistance, Mr. English directed me again to send out the memo. He said he wasn't going to change his mind about this mandate because he was a "legs man." I was appalled by his answer, so I went out that evening and purchased a pantsuit that I wore to work the following day. He was not happy with me, and he became disgruntled when some of the other teachers started wearing them, too.

In order to increase our enrollment, Mr. English obtained a grant that allowed boys who were expelled from public schools for their behavioral disorders, to attend our facility. This changed the whole atmosphere of our school. In the bathrooms, the businesspeople were intimidated by the boys who demanded money from them. These businesspeople were also distressed because the boys who were gay sometimes came to school dressed as females. In those cases, they weren't welcome in either the men's or the women's bathroom. There were so many complaints that management warned Mr. English he would be evicted from the building if he couldn't control this situation.

Mr. English found a vacant convent that was available for rent, so all the public school students were transferred there. This should have been an ideal situation because the nuns' bedrooms were perfect for private classrooms. However, the boys used these small rooms to attempt raping the teachers.

I was sent there to supervise the school, but I was told that under no circumstance was I to call the police for any student's misbehavior. *That wouldn't look good for the school.* However, there were so many threats and fights, even with guns and knives that I told Mr. English I couldn't handle the situation by myself. He said I should give the new situation a chance to develop. Due to my convent training, I thought I couldn't challenge him.

One day I was at my wits end, and I did call the police—which greatly displeased Mr. English. Three boys were chasing one another through the halls, and up and down the stairs. They were threatening to kill the one they caught. I took these threats very seriously.

Sister Maria helped me realize I had a right to make some demands, too. Just because this was my first job, I didn't need to accept, without discussion, that I was placed in a dangerous situation. I needed more help, and I had to have the authority to call the police when necessary.

When I threatened to quit, Mr. English finally hired Pete, a wrestler, to assist with these unruly boys. However, even Pete couldn't control them. When two boys were rolling on my desk with knives, I called Mr. English and asked him to come to my aid. He said, "Oh no … I won't go there until after the kids are gone." Here he was, the big former Marine, afraid of the boys—but he was perfectly willing to leave me there to deal with them.

None of the teachers stayed at that school very long. In fact, some left before their first day ended. I could no longer employ certified teachers, so I started using college students. Even they wouldn't stay! My final alternative was to use *anyone* who would make an attempt to teach them something. I was hoping that representatives from the Illinois State Board of Education would make a visit. They would have closed down the school immediately. When our grant wasn't renewed the next year, I was elated.

Since we were no longer renting the convent, I returned

to work in the office. I was still expected to complete lengthy projects, and Mr. English continued putting them in a pile on his desk. This was annoying because he always indicated it was imperative to complete these projects quickly.

When Mr. English was so demanding, and he wouldn't listen to reason, I started noting that sometimes he followed almost as many rules as there were in my Community: He was often just as demanding as my superiors; I was required to practice blind obedience when he gave me projects I knew he wouldn't use; and I couldn't show my feelings when he refused to discuss any issue.

Sometimes I came home from work feeling dirty. I was always glad when Sister Maria was there; I could count on getting a huge smile and a great big hug from her.

After leaving a difficult situation at school, it was a relief to come home and see the happy projects she was creating. There were the makings of candles in the kitchen. In the living room, she had velvet paintings, crocheting, sewing materials, writing projects, recipes, and music scattered about the room. She explained how each project would be used, and it was always to bring joy to others.

After Sister Maria's explanation about each item, I actually enjoyed seeing what looked like a mess in our living room. Her energy was boundless! Her goal was to bring peace and joy to everyone. If I wanted an area of neatness, I went to my bedroom to read, play music, pray, and enjoy the lake that was on the next block.

Obviously, I didn't complain to my superiors about my awful situation at work because I didn't want them to bring me back to Community living. Sister Maria and I prayed together regularly, and I came to the conclusion that if God wanted me in that position, it was up to me to accept what I couldn't change and change what I could. Sister Maria was such a blessing in my life. She helped me see the positive things I was doing, and she supported me in every way possible.

Unfortunately, two years later, Sister Maria received a grant at a large out of state university. I was devastated! Within a month, she was on her way to her newest challenge. I was left alone with all my good memories of her. Many times I cried myself to sleep because I missed her so much.

I never liked alcohol, but after Sister Maria left, I was so distressed that I purchased a gallon bottle of wine. I drank two glasses to relax. That was the beginning of a long series of alcoholic issues.

My checks from the tutoring company started bouncing, so I made the decision to retire from the school. When I told Mr. English I was leaving, he begged me to stay. He offered me many incentives, but I said he'd taken advantage of me once too often, and I needed more peace in my life than he could offer. I felt good about telling him this because he had lied to me several times, and I could no longer trust him.

19
Chapter

CONSIDERING EXCLAUSTRATION

Meanwhile, Sister Mary Lois said I couldn't live alone anymore, so I would be returning to a convent shortly. That was the last thing I wanted! She did say that if I could get another Sister to live with me, I would be able to stay there. I spoke to many Sisters, but none of them was interested in apartment living.

I told Sister Mary Lois I fulfilled my religious duties better in this type of environment, I seldom missed my prayer hour, and I felt closer to God because I wasn't living under rigid rules. Since I had a vow of obedience, she said I was obliged to follow her directives. She gave me a choice: either conform to her ruling or plan to leave the Community.

I was overwhelmed—after twenty-eight years in the Community, I could be dismissed so easily. That year, I spent a lot of time with Sister Mary Lois through letters and face-to-face meetings. She was adamant about her decision regarding my lifestyle. Through a great deal of prayer, I finally decided I was under too much stress, and it would be better for me to leave the Community. However, Sister Mary Lois asked me to take another year to consider my decision. I did this while still maintaining residence in my apartment.

Again, I was in close contact with Sister Mary Lois, but after completing another year of prayer and discernment, I was still unable to accept her ultimatum of blind obedience. I could not return to the stifling situation of rigid convent living!

Sister Mary Lois said I'd had every chance to obey her ultimatum. Since I was still not ready to accept it, my only alternative would be exclaustration. She provided me with an explanation of this serious proclamation.

> Exclaustration is a two-year period of prayer and discernment for a nun with perpetual vows who lives apart from the Community to decide whether she wants to return to the Community or sever her relations definitively.

I despondently accepted this proposal, knowing I was still bound by my religious vows and obligations. I was mandated to make a monthly appointment with a priest to discuss my pending departure from the Community.

I couldn't sleep because I knew exclaustration would lead to taking back the promises I made to God when I took my vows. I would be a *bad person.* Since I was having so much difficulty trying to sleep, my drinking escalated from an occasional drink to several drinks every evening.

1978: Petition to Sever Community Ties

Father Peterson was my counselor. He was assigned to confirm that I was fully aware of what my decision to leave the Community would entail. He gave me literature to read, and we discussed the pros and cons of my decision. He asked such questions as:

- Would you be able to give up your vows without tormenting yourself with guilt and imagined failure?
- Is your resistance to blind obedience because you vacillated between passive obedience and retaliation?
- Do you feel emotionally distraught?
- Do you accept that anger is a valid response to injustice?

After we had several discussions, Father Peterson said he'd have no problem submitting my severance papers to Rome for approval. He knew I was emotionally stable, and I understood the parameters of my Community separation.

20

Chapter

BUSINESS WORLD: 1976–1980

1976–1978: Publishing Company

Before I left the tutoring school, I interviewed for an editing position at an educational publishing company. I spoke with Ray, their sales manager. He was "laid-back", making me feel very comfortable. I learned later that this was his technique for obtaining personal information from applicants.

When he studied my résumé, he could see I was a teacher. However, I didn't tell him I was a nun because I didn't think it was relevant information for the editing position I was seeking. I was ready for questions about my teaching credentials, but I wasn't prepared to answer those about my Catholic background. He noted I had attended a Catholic high school, a Catholic college, and a Catholic university. Then I realized he suspected I was a nun.

He asked me where I'd taught. I named the first place that came to my mind: New Mexico. He questioned me about where the school was located in the city. I didn't know how to answer his question because, when we were on our missions, we knew all about our neighborhoods, but we were seldom allowed to explore the rest of the town. I tried to fake a response, but I wasn't very successful.

When I left the interview, I knew I hadn't done well. I kept reviewing what happened, and I came to the conclusion that even though I couldn't answer some of his questions, Ray seemed to like me. I felt sure he'd call me later.

Within a few weeks, I did hear from Ray. He said he had a good position that might interest me. It paid well, but there would be a lot of driving. When I told him I didn't know how to drive, he was astounded, but he reluctantly said the position obviously wasn't appropriate for me.

When I realized that, because I didn't drive, I'd lost a good job opportunity, I decided to take driving lessons. I spent many hours on the road with a driving instructor, and within a week I had my license. I contacted Ray and said I'd like to take him to lunch to discuss future employment with the company. He was so impressed that I'd taken driving lessons, he readily agreed to my invitation.

A week after our lunch, I was contacted by the publisher's director of human resources. She told me about a position where I would edit a book on reading skills, authored by one of their well-known writers. I was delighted to obtain this excellent position. Although the job was quite interesting, I found the author to be eccentric, and she wasn't the easiest person to satisfy. However, when her book was ready for publication, she thanked me profusely and asked if I might edit her next book. I was honored, particularly since I'd never done professional editing before.

She wasn't ready for her next book to be edited, so I was assigned to assist with a new spelling series that was being prepared for publication—grades one through eight. Ray frequently came to my cubicle to see how things were going. I had no idea he was a vice president until my coworkers asked me why he was so interested in what I was doing. When I told them he interviewed me, they were curious, because ordinarily, all interviews were arranged by human resources. (I never did know why I interviewed with Ray instead of going through the normal channels of employment.)

One afternoon, Ray called me aside to say I'd just received a promotion. I was to be the new advertising manager, and he would be my supervisor. I was reluctant to accept this position since I had no experience in advertising. However, he convinced me it wouldn't be too difficult, and he'd be there to assist me.

A large part of my responsibilities was to supply our forty-seven sales representatives with any books or other materials they needed for their territories. In the past, they had requested these items, but they never received them. It took some time to convince the representatives that our team would do our best to supply their needs. My staff of three prepared these mailings daily.

I depended on Art, the owner of our advertising company, to assist me in developing ideas for brochures appropriate for mailings to all schools. He always had wonderful concepts, and since I wrote the copy for many of these promotions, he always gave me a fair amount of credit for their production.

Another of my tasks was to write a monthly newsletter, advising the salespeople about successful techniques used by other representatives. This entailed contact with many representatives who were more than willing to provide any information I needed.

The main focus of our education department was a revised edition of a social studies series for grades one through eight.

The salespeople were always delighted when I traveled to their book fairs because they knew I had used most of these books myself. The teachers at the conference were impressed when I demonstrated unique methods for utilizing various sections of the books. Since I was a teacher, rather than a salesperson, the teachers were usually favorably impressed with my presentation. This led to good book sales.

When I met with any of the representatives out of state, Ray told me to always take them to one of the finest restaurants in the city. He knew they wouldn't be reimbursed if they dined in their own territory, but if I took them out, I would be compensated when I turned in my expense account.

At first, the representatives were reluctant to accept my dinner invitation. However, when I explained that Ray told me to pick up the tab, they always suggested wonderful restaurants. During the meal, they told me all about their territories, and they expressed their appreciation for the support our team gave them.

However, Ray was aghast when he learned that one of the reps chose to take me to a Bunny Club. I was intrigued with the atmosphere, but as one might surmise, I was extremely uncomfortable in those surroundings. I couldn't wait to leave.

Wine was no longer strong enough to help me sleep, so I was now drinking vodka. Because I didn't know how quickly the alcohol would affect me, I never drank with the representatives. I waited until I returned to my hotel room.

At our company, we were all treated like family; even though we were in different departments, most of us knew each other. If someone needed help, we were right there to assist in any way we could, even if that person wasn't in our department. Our newsletter reflected our supervisors' appreciation for our efforts to make our company the best ever.

One morning, the entire staff was summoned for an important meeting. We knew there was a search in progress for a new company president, but we had no idea the search was over. We were introduced to John Peterson, our new company president. He said we had always been a family-owned business, but he was going to convert it to a *slick* operation. What a disappointment!

Michelle, a marketing director, was now my supervisor. I was obviously disappointed that I'd no longer have close contact with Ray. Michelle was a bit flighty. She often told me to prepare a project, and then she changed her mind while I was in the middle of it. She contacted Art at the advertising agency without telling me her plan; yet she expected me to follow through with it.

I became frustrated, as did Art. He had worked with our company for many years, and he knew that some of Michelle's ideas were cost-prohibitive. Sometimes, when she was persistent, Art contacted Ray to confirm the feasibility of her plan. In most cases, her projects were dropped.

Michelle started firing people, including my assistants. She claimed it wasn't cost-effective to allow the salespeople to have free rein with their requests. I guess she didn't realize they were the *bread and butter* of the company.

Art had other educational clients, so I asked him to watch for an appropriate position for me; I knew Michelle would fire me next. Art claimed, "They'll never fire you. You're too valuable to them."

However, that Friday afternoon, Michelle called me into her office and told me they no longer had a need for someone with my talents. She said I should leave immediately, not stop in my office, and not talk to anyone on the way out. These directives were impossible! Although I had started bringing things home,

I needed to collect my purse and some other personal items. I also wanted to send a note to the representatives to let them know their requests would now be greatly curtailed.

When my coworkers saw me crying, word spread quickly throughout the company that I had been fired. Within ten minutes, about twenty furious people assembled outside my door. They were loud in their criticism of Michelle, and they developed an attitude of rebellion toward her.

The salespeople were also upset when they heard I was dismissed. Some of them wrote to thank me for all I did for them. Their messages included the following:

- "I would be happy to write you a letter of recommendation."
- "There aren't enough words in the English language to thank you."
- "It is a great disappointment that you will no longer be with us."
- "Your contributions were very professional and valuable."
- "Your letter to the representatives came as a disappointment."
- "You have left a position that gave all of us everything we needed."

After I was fired, I called Art to let him know what happened. He couldn't believe she had let me go. He said he had a prospective new client; if his proposal was accepted, he would have a position for me at his agency. He said he'd have this information by Wednesday. I was so devastated that I'd been fired; I went home and got drunk.

Shortly after I was fired, I was hostess for a group of eight nuns from various Communities. We met once a month in each other's homes. We all brought a dish so it wouldn't be too difficult for the hostess to prepare dinner. When we could get one of the priests to come, we had Mass; otherwise, we had a simple prayer session along with good conversation and laughter. These nuns were delightful! They each worked in various community programs, so they had a lot to talk about.

When the group met at my apartment, several of the Sisters brought alcoholic beverages along with the dish they'd prepared. I didn't drink any alcohol while they were there. However, they left open bottles on the kitchen counter, so the minute they departed, I started guzzling the liquor. One Sister called from the lobby to say she'd left her scarf in my apartment. By the time she came upstairs, I was already unsteady on my feet.

1978–1980: Advertising Agency

Art did obtain the contract for his new client, so he hired me at his agency. He said he was delighted to have me aboard because we had worked together through the publishing company; he knew I was knowledgeable and a good employee. He appreciated my writing skills, and he gave me many opportunities to write for large projects.

Because our agency was small, the phone was answered by whoever was near it. Several times when Michelle phoned, I received the call, but I never indicated who I was. She was usually frantic because she had neglected to set up a project that was needed within the next few days. Because of her oversights, the charges from the design department and the printer's fees for overtime were exorbitant.

When she discovered Art had employed me, she called to ask if I'd return to the publishing company. She said she had acted in haste. She offered to increase my salary substantially, and there would be many other benefits. Of course I refused her offer.

She called a second time, offering me even more incentives. She probably made these offers because the salespeople voiced their strong objections to my dismissal. I think Michelle was trying to cover her mistake. She was obviously in big trouble. Of course I refused her offer again.

Art was fuming when he heard what she was doing. He called her and said she should discontinue her efforts to entice me with bonuses. I had assured him that under no circumstances did I want to return to that company.

Michelle lasted three months at the publishing company, and then she was fired. Meanwhile, she left a path of devastation behind her.

I loved working at the advertising agency, and Art appreciated my effort and enthusiasm. When I wasn't writing or editing, I worked on small jobs no one else had taken the time to do. One of my major projects was to organize our messy file cabinets. We had a drawer for each client, but everything was just thrown into it with no files. When Art was with a prospective client, he frequently asked me to bring him a particular brochure. Sometimes it took me a little while to find it due to the disorganization.

Art was delighted when I proposed to get the drawers systemized. However, Bud, the art director, was very negative about this endeavor. He had been employed at the agency for many years, and he had his own way of doing things. He had piles of projects on top the file cabinets. Even though no one else knew his system, he could quickly find anything he needed.

He kept complaining that there was no need for all the new files because he knew exactly where everything was. Whenever he saw me working on the files, he made negative comments about the project. He said, "Ever since you came into the office, you've been trying to change everything." However, after the files were finished, he admitted it was easier for all of us to find what we needed.

One of my major responsibilities was to proofread copy the printer sent over to us. I returned it to him with corrections. Sometimes he called me and said he couldn't read my copy changes. When I looked at my own copy, I couldn't read them either; my hands were shaky due to my drinking.

Even though I was drinking regularly, I was ordinarily able to fulfill my job requirements; however times like this made me realize I needed to be more careful. Although I was on exclaustration, I was still a nun, so no one suspected that a nun would be drinking, especially because I was a high-functioning alcoholic.

I had always been an organized person, but I started to avoid filing invoices and billing receipts. When anyone looked for them, it was a surprise that I hadn't recorded and filed them properly. This was another signal for me to correct this matter as quickly as possible so no one would suspect I was disorganized due to my drinking. Instead of facing my problem, I did everything I could to cover it up.

21

Chapter

ALCOHOLISM: DENIAL AND ACCEPTANCE

Purchasing my alcohol was quite an experience. Since my name, Sister Mary, was printed on my checks, I always told the salespeople at the liquor store I was having a party. When I was checking out my purchases, they'd often say, "Another party, Sister?" Sometimes when I walked into the store, they would call very loudly, "Hi, Sister!" I figured I was becoming too well-known at that store. Since I now needed vodka more often, I started going to other stores, never the same ones.

Every morning, I had a hangover. I promised myself I wouldn't drink that night... but I did! At that point, I had no control over my addiction. It had gotten to be extremely difficult for me to get to work, but I knew I had to be there, if for no other reason, than not wanting anyone to know about my dependence on alcohol.

Many days, I didn't remember taking the bus to work. Until later in the morning, I didn't even know if I was wearing clean clothes. One day when I was standing near the copier, I looked down at my shoes and realized they didn't match. Surprisingly, no one at work realized I was in jeopardy because they never thought a nun would be an alcoholic.

One Sunday afternoon, I was so sick that I couldn't drag myself to the store to purchase my vodka, so I called for a delivery. This vodka cost me twenty-five dollars, but I needed it, no matter what the cost. I knew I had a problem, but I had no idea how serious it was.

If I made an error at work, it was chalked up to the fact that I was overwhelmed with too many projects. It was always overlooked because almost everything else I did was perfect. I had no idea how many medical concerns I was facing.

I was drinking a lot of vodka every night. I thought if I stopped drinking by ten o'clock, I would be okay the next morning. Later, I changed the time to eleven o'clock. ... then midnight . ... then one o'clock a.m. Eventually, there were nights when I drank so much, I didn't sleep at all.

It was getting more difficult to get up and function well at work. Although I had always arrived at the office early and stayed late, I began coming in later because I couldn't get ready on time. When I was actually late for work, I started lying, but I couldn't even keep my lies straight. I told the receptionist my bus was late; I went right into the art director's office and claimed I'd had a long distance call; and finally, I told Art I'd spilled my coffee and had to change my clothes. (I don't even drink coffee!)

Although I had no Idea I was having blackouts that was exactly what was happening to me:

- One morning, when I went to the kitchen, I found three empty containers from TV dinners. I had no idea if I'd cooked them or eaten them raw.

- Another day I found an empty Jell-O box on the kitchen counter. Apparently I'd run out of diet soda and used that to sweeten my vodka.

- I must have mopped the kitchen floor one night because in the morning a bucket of water and my mop were sitting there.

I had an appointment with my internist one Saturday morning. He was concerned that my blood pressure was so high. I never told him I was drinking because I didn't realize it was a medical issue. He gave me a prescription which I brought to Walgreen's. While I was waiting for it to be filled, I noticed they had vodka on sale: three bottles for ten dollars. I decided to take advantage of the sale, so I purchased three bottles.

During the Christmas holidays, Art always had a party for his clients. I was usually the first one there to prepare for any celebration. When I didn't appear at the office, he thought maybe my bus was late, and I'd be coming in before long.

That morning, the clients arrived about eleven o'clock. When they asked where I was, Art told them I was delayed, but he hoped I would be there shortly. Our secretary called my home, but there was no answer. After she called several times, she became concerned, so she called my building manager. When he went upstairs to my apartment, he found my door bolted and the TV blaring, so he called the police. They cut the lock and found me lying on the floor, unconscious; I was surrounded by pills. Apparently, in my blackout, I remembered I had new blood pressure pills to take. I must have spilled them when I fell. The police didn't know what these pills were, so they surmised I was trying to commit suicide. When they looked around my apartment, they found three empty vodka bottles. Obviously, when I was in a blackout, I drank all three of them between Saturday afternoon and Sunday evening.

The paramedics were called, and while I was still unconscious, I was taken to the closest hospital where they pumped my stomach. The doctor who performed this procedure told me I was an alcoholic and needed help. I was actually relieved that someone finally knew my secret about drinking, but I wasn't ready to admit I was an alcoholic.

Since my family lived in Florida, Art came to the hospital and spoke with the doctor to see how he could help me. He was told that in order for me to begin my recovery, I needed to go through a rehabilitation program. I said I didn't need such a plan because it wouldn't happen again.

Art was insistent that I attend the program. I started making excuses, such as "I can't afford it," but he said my insurance would cover it, and he would pay me for the time I was away. He had an answer for every excuse I gave. He finally said if I didn't go to rehab, I wouldn't have a job. That did it! However, I made up my mind that when I got there, I would prove I wasn't an alcoholic.

I was scheduled to visit my mother in Florida the next day, but the doctor said I was too ill to travel. I called my sister to let her know what happened. My mother had been a nurse, so she understood physical issues. Colleen told her my blood pressure was too high for me to travel. However, if she knew her daughter-the-nun was going to an alcohol treatment center, Mom would have been devastated.

I was still on exclaustration, so when I was filling out my admission papers, I made it clear that no one, other than the staff, was to know I was a nun. Then I went to my room where one of the nurses greeted me by saying, "Welcome to our program. My name is Lois, and I'm an alcoholic." I thought, "They even let *those* people have good jobs." It seemed that I couldn't get it through my head that I was an alcoholic, too.

I spent the first week at the rehab trying to prove I wasn't an alcoholic. I smiled all the time and walked up and down the halls offering to help everyone in any way I could. I even helped clean up the kitchen. The staff was concerned because I wasn't getting in touch with myself and recognizing I had a serious problem. Until I did that, recovery wasn't possible.

Part of the program was for us to meet with a counselor in small groups of five or six people. After a few of these sessions, Rita, the therapist who directed our group, said I had something to tell the others. I insisted I had nothing to say, but she was persistent. After she told me several times that it was imperative for me to tell my secret, I finally said, "Okay, I'm a nun."

One of the men looked disgusted and said, "I don't care what you are. You're an alcoholic just like the rest of us!"

That was the beginning of my recovery! I finally realized I wasn't better than anyone else, and I wasn't a special person. From that time on, I participated fully in the program, and I was willing to accept all the help being showered on me.

After three weeks, I was scheduled to leave the hospital. I went home on Valentine's Day, a day that seemed appropriate for me to start my journey of recovery.

I was determined to follow the program, just as I'd been taught. My plan was to attend AA recovery meetings, find a sponsor, and stay in touch with the "winners." I did just that, **and** today *I have forty years of sobriety.*

As I've been taught in AA, my material goods may not be great, but I have a fortune in friendship. Best of all, I have the love and understanding of a gracious God who allows me to reap the rewards that come from loving and assisting others and allowing them to love and assist me.

After I left rehab, Art was concerned that if I went home alone, I might be tempted to drink again, so he invited me to stay with his family. He had a mother-in-law apartment in his home that wasn't being used, so that's where I stayed. When we drove to and from work together, it was an opportunity for us to discuss various office projects.

After two weeks, I told Art how much I appreciated his concern for me, but it was time for me to go home. He really didn't want me to leave, but I knew my apartment was a mess, and I needed to start cleaning it. I will never forget how good he was to me.

Art stayed in touch with the doctors at the rehab. They told him it was crucial for me to attend AA meetings daily. Since our office was located in the city's downtown area, there were many noon meetings attended by businesspeople.

Art directed me to join these meetings regularly. Although this would extend my lunch period, that didn't matter to him. He just wanted me to be well.

After I left Art's home, it was time for me to reestablish myself in my apartment complex. Many residents had seen me carried out of our building on a stretcher. It didn't take long for everyone to know I had overdosed on alcohol and had spent several weeks in rehabilitation. When they saw me, many of the residents were embarrassed because they didn't know what to say to me. It was my responsibility to put them at ease and let them know I was home, and I was getting well.

The night I left Art's home, the board pf directors was having a wine and cheese party for the residents. Since I'd missed so many activities while I was gone, I decided to attend this gathering—which was not really the smartest thing for me to do under the circumstances. When people arrived, they were offered wine, soda, or water. When I arrived, I was just offered soda or water. (I was aware that most residents were watching what I drank.) Later on, I spoke to the hostess and assured her that I knew she had the best of intentions when she didn't offer me any wine, but *she* made a decision not to offer it to me instead of allowing me to make my own decision. My friends all wanted to help me, but it was my responsibility to educate them to the fact that I needed to make my own choices.

Art was a great man After all the wonderful things he did for me, as well as for many others, our whole staff was devastated when he lost three of his major clients. He said he could no longer maintain his business without these clients, so he advised us to look for new jobs. He even said we could make all the phone calls we needed, and he'd give us company time for interviews. However, none of us took his recommendations seriously, because we hoped things would improve, and we could all stay with him.

It broke his heart when he had to start letting us go. I was the first one dismissed because my major jobs were writing and editing. Since he was a good writer, he could fulfil any needed writing or editing job himself. I was sad, but I understood why he had to give me notice.

22
Chapter

FINAL EXCLAUSTRATION

About that time, in 1980, my approval papers to permanently separate myself from the Community arrived from Rome. Father Peterson called to say my request was official. He had counseled me during the past two years, but he was required to ask me again if I still wanted to separate myself from my Community forever.

Although I had now been in the Community for over thirty years, I strongly affirmed my decision to leave. He gave me some papers to sign, and from that time on *I was no longer a nun.* I felt empty! It was all over! Did I fail? No. I knew I could no longer live where I was stifled and required to accept blind obedience. I knew I could no longer get "hurt" because I was being transferred from convent to convent. I knew I no longer needed to be a people-pleaser for people I disliked. I also knew I could still do God's work wherever I went, not necessarily in a convent.

After I signed my separation papers with Father Peterson, I met with Sister Mary Lois who gave me $1,000 and told me the Community would no longer assume any responsibility for my well-being. **I was on my own.**

Because I could no longer afford the rent for the apartment where I'd been living, I moved to a different complex. For my new apartment, I needed, among other things: furniture, drapes, dishes, and a carpet. I picked up some small things at a thrift shop, and my cousin and some of his friends donated other major items to the "cause". I ended up with a black couch, a red rug, and orange drapes, which actually looked very nice together.

Before I made any other commitments, my first priority was my AA recovery program; it is one of the most important involvements in my life. I thank God every day for this wonderful program that literally saved my life. My spiritual life, enriched by my AA recovery program, brings me closer to God every day. I can now see the wonders of nature again: the flowers, the green grass, and the different types of clouds. I can also enjoy reading books again and joining my friends for an evening of entertainment. Once again I can volunteer at organizations to help the needy in many capacities.

I talk to God every morning, and He stays with me throughout the day. I ask Him for the courage, strength, and wisdom to be the person He wants me to be. It's a good feeling to know He loves me just the way I am.

My prayer-life includes spiritual reading and devotions that enhance my relationship with my God. One of my favorite prayers is the *Serenity Prayer* by Reinhold Niebuhr:

> God, grant me the serenity
> to accept the things I cannot change,
> the courage to change the things I can,
> and the wisdom to know the difference.

I've been asked if, after I left the Community, I severed ties with the Church. I never thought about leaving the Church! In fact, just as always, I was very active in my parish. I was a Communion minister, lector (*reader*), choir member, and usher. I made myself available for any project where assistance was needed. I loved participating in parish activities, and I loved working with neighborhood communities in several capacities.

I've also been asked if I ever had a male friend after I left the convent. The answer is, "Yes!" Amin lived in the same building where I swam. He was in the pool every day, so I started talking with him. When I tell my friends the first thing I said to him was, "I really admire your breath control," I give them a good laugh.

At one time, Amin had a very high position in an eastern country. However, a new regime tried to execute all members of the previous administration so they could have a purified society. Amin was unable to leave his country legally, so he began hiding in friends' attics, and even at his ex-wife's home. After a year of exile, he decided this was no way to live, so he planned an escape to the United States. He had only a 10 percent chance of survival, but he was willing to take that gamble.

Through an underground strategy, he trudged over the mountain into a more friendly country. He had a horse for the last ten miles of his trip, but the horse fell in mud, and Amin's ankle was broken. He was so determined to get to his destination that he walked the distance on his injured ankle. He was given a false passport so he could continue to travel. He eventually reached the United States where he kissed the ground upon his arrival.

Amin was a true gentleman. We enjoyed spending time together. He told me he had seen the movie, *Amadeus.* I said I hoped to see it eventually; he asked me if I would accompany him to see it again. I really enjoyed the film, but I was amused when he covered my eyes for scenes he didn't think were appropriate for me to see.

When he discovered that I liked movies, Amin invited me to see *Gandhi*, another film he had already seen. From there, our friendship developed to where we loved each other as very good friends. We both knew nothing more than that could ever be possible since he hoped to eventually return to his country and his family.

Amin respected me, and he never put me in an uncomfortable position. We spent many weekend afternoons visiting nearby states and finding new restaurants. I didn't realize the custom in his country was to never allow a woman to pay for anything if she was with a man. The first time we went to lunch, I tried to take the check. He was insulted, and he told me to never open my purse when I was with him.

Through a great effort on the part of our American Embassy, Amin eventually returned to his country where politics and a great deal of money allowed him to return from exile.

Later, when I moved to Florida, Amin tried to call me twice, but I wasn't home to get his call. Unfortunately, I didn't have his phone number because his overseas number wasn't recorded on my phone. I do have an old phone number of his that I could use in an attempt to call him; however, women are not supposed to call men, so I fear I might cause a problem if I call. I'm sure he has tried to call me again, but I've changed phones, and I have a new number. I've asked several people who speak Farsi to try to call him, and at least find out if he is still living; he would now be ninety-five years old. Because of their fear of the regime, no one is willing to call.

As far as the Community was concerned, I thought it might be nice to stay in contact with former Sisters so we could pray and socialize together. I wrote to the superiors twice to request a list of these women; I never received an answer. However, even though *my* efforts weren't successful, that plan did eventually come to fruition: a group of former Sisters established an affiliation with the Community so they could maintain relationships with other Sisters who had left their Community ministry. They meet regularly, and they try to have summer reunions at the motherhouse every three to five years. I always receive an invitation to this gathering, but at the thought of returning to the motherhouse, my stomach starts churning. I'm not ready to attend now, and I'm not sure I ever will be ready.

The first time I was contacted by the Community was a year after I left when they sent a request for a fundraising donation. I was not a "happy camper." I wrote to them saying I didn't appreciate receiving this request as my first communication with them. I said they had no idea what my finances were; yet they felt free to make a request for funding. To their credit, I was sent a letter of apology.

23
Chapter

...AND LIFE GOES ON

1980–1981: State University, Department of Child Development

After I left the Community and lost my job at the advertising agency, I started a job search. Fortunately, I didn't need to explore my options very long. One of my friends was a director in the Department of Child Development at a large university. He spoke very highly of me to another director in that department, so I was invited for an interview.

Katherine knew I was sixty-five years old when she hired me, but she had full confidence I was qualified to be her assistant. She and I made a great team. She was appreciative of everything I did, and she didn't hesitate to tell me. She was the best supervisor I ever had!

Since I was a people-pleaser, recognition from her fed into my desire to take on even more responsibilities. My goal was to assist Katherine in any way I could by relieving her of some of her many duties. I volunteered for projects that had been neglected for many years: developing a phone directory of the doctors and residents in four buildings; taking inventory of all furniture and computers in every office; and cleaning out rooms where old furniture had been stored. I undertook projects in many other areas, too, and I was soon in charge of writing orders for painters, carpenters, movers, and the maintenance staff to service our department as needed. These workers were very willing to assist me because I always let them know how much I appreciated their service, and I often sent complimentary notes to their supervisors. Sometimes I even provided refreshments for them while they were working. They were grateful for my efforts, and they were willing to do almost anything I asked of them—even to come in on a Saturday when inspectors were due within the week.

Some of the doctors had no secretary, so they asked if I would assist them, too. They gave me letters to type and grants to edit. I was very happy in my job, and I was always willing to assist people wherever I could. I was extremely busy, but I couldn't wait to get to work each morning. Unfortunately, after a year, Katherine was fired. I was devastated!

Since the person for this job would be second in command in the largest department of the university, I presumed there would be a long search. However, the person they quickly selected for this position was Tony, a young man who was a special friend of Dr. Joe, head of the department.

Except for their friendship, no one could understand Dr. Joe's decision. Tony had been an IT assistant; he had no experience in management, budgets, or major decisions regarding building acquisitions. He frequently made bad judgments.

Tony became my new supervisor. I had six different job titles, so I tried to have weekly meetings with him. However, he seldom took the time to talk with me. It was frustrating when he said, "You're doing a great job. Just continue doing what you're doing."

When it came time for reviews, I asked him when I would have mine. He kept putting me off, saying he'd get to it soon. He never did, so when the report on salary increases was available to supervisors, I asked him if he would at least tell me what my pay raise would be. Since he had actually been one of the "budget makers," I was unhappy when he said he couldn't remember.

When payday arrived, my check showed that I'd received a $300 raise for the entire year. I knew this was inconceivable because of all the work I produced, so I told him this was an insult, and I would be searching for a job in another department. He asked me to give him a chance to make it good. However, after many unsatisfactory meetings with him and Dr. Joe, I finally left the department for a position in the Department of Pharmacy. Since I really loved my job in the Department of Child Development, I actually "cut off my nose to spite my face."

1981: Macular Degeneration

Before I left the Department of Child Development, I'd been in the process of developing a technical computer chart. When the lines of the graph suddenly seemed to curve, I thought something was wrong with my computer, so I called the IT staff to take a look at it. They said nothing was wrong with my computer; it had to be a problem with my eyes.

I called Dr. Murphy, my ophthalmologist, and explained the situation to him. He said I should come into his office immediately. Since it was already four o'clock, and it would take me at least an hour to get there, I knew there was no way I could reach his office before he closed it for the day; he was kind enough to wait for me.

When I arrived, Dr. Murphy immediately examined my

eyes. He said I needed to see a retina specialist without delay. He called his friend, Dr. Swanson, at home. I was told to come to his office the next morning at nine o'clock.

After his examination was completed, Dr. Swanson's diagnosis was that I had macular degeneration. He explained that within a short time, I would have only peripheral vision in my left eye, and eventually I would lose most of the sight in it.

For two months, Dr. Swanson examined my eyes weekly. My condition did not improve, so he believed a laser treatment would be the best option available.

At that time, this treatment was considered the *gold standard*. Today, due to extensive research, it is now one of the lowest treatments on the totem pole. There are many new alternatives, but because I had the laser treatment, where my blood cells were cauterized, I am not eligible to participate in any of them.

When I have my eyes examined today, I can't even see the large E with my left eye. Fortunately, my right eye is strong enough that I'm still able to do daytime driving.

Copywriting and editing were my specialties, but they are no longer an option for me. In order to be sure I've checked everything correctly, I must increase the type size and use my magnifying glass to proofread documents.

I had been an avid reader. At first, I felt deprived of this pleasure. However, I discovered the *Nook*, where I can make the type size as large as I need. Now I am still an avid reader!

1981–1982: State University, Department of Pharmacy

When I started working in the Department of Pharmacy with Dr. Stone, I found he was a perfectionist and a very difficult person to please. He expected me to produce more work than I could possibly deliver, so he became annoyed and started nitpicking everything I did. Although my salary was low, he frequently told me they paid me too much for incompetent work. I was devastated when he made such remarks. We had a meeting every morning, and I always received negative comments such as the following:

- I didn't answer the phone on the first ring.
- I took too long to have the dean sign grants. (*Sometimes she was on the phone or in conference, so I couldn't interrupt her.*)
- When I carried blood samples to a nearby hospital, I didn't return quickly enough to complete my other responsibilities.
- I worked overtime, so I obviously wasn't organized enough to finish my work during regular work hours.
- I didn't get his white coats to the laundry quickly enough.
- I paged him when he was having a conference with the dean because his wife called to say there was an emergency at home.
- I didn't get his travel vouches reimbursed quickly enough. (*I had to wait until the finance department had them ready.*)
- When he gave me two major jobs to do, he expected to have them both completed that day. (*This was impossible, so when I asked him which one he needed first, he said, "Both of them."*)

I usually ended up in tears throughout the day. Other doctors in the department kept telling me they appreciated all I did, and I shouldn't let him ruin my day. However, they worked *under* Dr. Stone, so they didn't want to get involved with him about the way he treated me.

Eventually, when I saw my internist again and he saw how

distressed I was, he said that if I didn't leave that job in the near future, he would admit me to a psychiatric hospital. At that point, I was ready to go!

I had lots of vacation and sick time available, so when our church choir was invited to Rome to sing at one of the pope's celebrations, I went with them. What an experience! We arrived in Rome on December 26, and we were scheduled to sing the following morning. When we reached the basilica (*the pope's church*), we were delighted to see that our choir's designated spot was right in front of the pope's ornate altar. However, our delight changed to disappointment when we found he no longer used that altar because he was unable to climb the stairs. He sat on a side area of the basilica.

Some of our choir members had long-range cameras, so we have many pictures of the pope that were taken during the Service. After Mass, the pope came around the entire church in his popemobile. He stopped about every seventy-five feet to bless those in that area. It was a huge spiritual experience!

While I was in Rome, I prayed for guidance regarding my job. I peacefully decided I would retire, effective February 1. That was no surprise to anyone in our department. Although I received checks for unused vacation and sick time, I never again returned to the university.

24
Chapter

LIFE IN RETIREMENT

Tutoring and Substitute Teaching

Because I was now retired, I needed to find sources of income. I couldn't count on Social Security because the Community had never paid enough into it, so for thirty years I had no benefits.

I accepted a position where I tutored a set of twins who had not been promoted to seventh grade because they were so far behind in every subject. Tom and Bob came to my home for two hours every day, five days each week. For the most part, they were on the same level for every subject, so they could easily be taught together. They related well to their one-on-one personal instructions. In fact, they did so well, they were accepted back at their old school for eighth grade. Their mother was delighted! She gave me a gold bracelet with a charm that read, "World's Greatest Teacher." I still have it today.

After the boys returned to school, I started doing substitute teaching at three neighboring Catholic schools. I learned some of their rules the hard way. When I went to pick up second-grade children from the lunchroom, one of the cafeteria mothers told me that Tim kept walking around, and he wouldn't sit down. I tapped him on his butt and scolded, "Now, sit down!" As far as I was concerned, the issue was closed. However, that afternoon, the principal came to my classroom to say I had touched Tim, and that should never happen again. I couldn't help but think about the good old days when punishments were far more severe.

To further increase my income, I did private tutoring in my home after school. Children came for one, two, or three days each week. On their scheduled days, I picked up two of them from school. I taught one child at three o'clock while the other one did homework. At four o'clock we switched places, and at five o'clock their parents came to pick them up.

This system worked well. The children liked coming to my apartment, and most of the residents enjoyed seeing their smiling faces. These children made huge strides in school, and they could hardly wait to show me their good papers. I formed some excellent relationships, not only with the children, but also with their parents. I still receive newsy emails from several of these parents. Their children are now adults in the business world where they are doing well. I always appreciate these updates so I can follow the students I tutored.

Christine was very special. She came from Romania in the middle of first grade, not knowing any English. Because of her lack of English skills, she wasn't ready for promotion to second grade. Her teachers said she would be held back, but her mother refused to accept that decision. She kept saying, "Christine is very smart!" The teachers decided that, since her mother was so adamant, the only way they'd consider promoting her would be if she was tutored all summer.

That's how I met Christine. Her grandmother brought her

to my home three days each week for an hour. I gave her lots of homework, and it was always completed. By the time school started, she was on a high first-grade level. She was still behind her class, but she continued to come for tutoring three days each week. She progressed well in second grade because she did all her schoolwork plus everything I assigned. When she realized what good progress she was making, she was even more motivated to succeed. She was *on level* when she entered third grade.

I tutored Christine until she graduated from eighth grade. She did so well in high school that she received a four-year scholarship for books and tuition at a large Catholic college. She proved her mother was right: Christine is very smart!

Apartment and Neighborhood Issues

I was no stranger to the experience of apartment living, but now I became more involved in the building activities: assisting with holiday parties, scheduling musical groups to perform for us, and developing a library for the building. Eventually, I was elected to the board of directors. This position had a lot of pros and cons. I could listen to complaints, and I could attempt to appease people, even though they were often inconsiderate and called me or knocked on my door at late hours. Sometimes I had to tell them the board would need to make a decision regarding their issue. This did not placate them; they became disgruntled and spread the word that the board was not listening to their problems.

However, being a board member made me one of the building's decision-makers. One of our first major decisions was to purchase the vacant lot next to our building at an attractive price. Since our garage was overcrowded, this acquisition would provide extended parking space for us. We thought this would be an *easy vote,* but some residents were not amenable to this purchase because their maintenance fees would be slightly increased. Sadly, we lost our bid to another buyer.

Another of the board's issues was to inform the residents that the building needed tuckpointing. There was no way this process could be delayed any longer. Again, many of our residents strenuously objected because they knew this would entail a large increase in their maintenance fees. The matter was finally resolved when both our lawyer and construction manager said if we refused any longer, our building would become a C-class building instead of an A. This would greatly reduce our property values.

On Easter Sunday I had a mishap. I'd been out all day and was exhausted when I returned home. I ran bathwater and fell asleep on the couch. When I woke up, I was walking in deep water.

I wasn't sure what to do because I had a very early medical appointment for a time-consuming test. Since I'd waited more than six weeks for this appointment, I knew I really had to keep it. However, I didn't want to leave the mess behind me, either. I asked our doorman to contact the supervisor of maintenance, who lived in the building and received a free apartment so he could be on call for emergencies.

Meanwhile, since I lived on the tenth floor, the water was running behind the pipes to every bathroom nine floors below me. Fortunately, the only bathroom damaged was the one on the second floor where the water had nowhere else to go; it poured out their bathroom vent. (I can't imagine what it would be like to walk into your bathroom and see a flood of water rushing out your vent!)

In the end it all worked out well. The building manager

checked the water pipes in the damaged bathroom, and he had the room painted. This was covered by my home insurance. My insurance also covered new carpeting in my living room and bedroom. They replaced the kitchen floor, and they even restored the wallpaper in my bathroom that was starting to peel before the flood.

When I told the insurance agent I'd empty the living room cabinets to make it easier to install the new carpet, the agent arranged to pay me $100 to empty two cabinets and another $100 to put everything back again.

I lived in this building for nine years, but I moved out after a serious incident occurred. Danny, a five-year old, was staying with me for the day. We decided to walk to the grocery store so I could cash a check. However, because it was Sunday, the store closed early, so I was unable to get the cash I wanted. Danny asked me if I had enough money to buy him some apple juice at the fruit store. I checked my wallet and saw that I had seventy-nine cents. The price of the juice was sixty-five cents, so I told him we could get it.

It was a beautiful afternoon. Danny was learning to read, so, as we walked, he would say, "That must say *gas station*, because it's a gas station. ... That must say *library*, because it's a library. ... That must say *restaurant*, because it's a restaurant." We were both enjoying ourselves, and we greeted everyone we met along the way.

Danny drank part of his apple juice, and then he asked me to hold the bottle. When we reached the corner near my apartment building, we greeted a young man who looked like he was waiting for a bus. However, as we walked a little farther, this fellow came from behind us and grabbed my shoulder bag. I struggled with him but the strap broke, so he had my purse.

When that happened, I lost my balance and fell down…and the juice bottle broke.

As he held my purse, the man turned around and said very loudly, **"Don't cut me!"** He scattered everything from my purse on the ground and ran off with my wallet. I still had my glasses, credit cards, driver's license, medical cards, and all the other paraphernalia I carried in my purse. (I'll bet he was surprised when he opened my wallet!)

Danny asked why the bad man did that. I tried to explain that some people want money, so they steal from others. His next question was, "Why don't they get a job and earn their own money?" Danny was full of questions that weren't readily answered. All he understood was: this was an injustice that needed to be made right.

When I discovered that Danny was staying with different people every night, I told his mother he could stay with me during the week. I brought him to kindergarten every morning and picked him up from daycare in the evening. This arrangement lasted for more than a year. (Her excuse for pawning him off every night was that she wanted to have *fun*. He was obviously in the way of her social life!)

Although she never reimbursed me for anything, his mother made rules we were supposed to follow. Danny was to be in bed by seven o'clock, and she said he was too old to have toys in the bathtub with him.

It wasn't possible to follow these regulations. I didn't leave work until five o'clock, and it was six o'clock before I could pick up Danny. Sometimes I needed to do a little shopping. By the time we came home, ate dinner and did the dishes together, it was long past seven o'clock. He liked it when I read to him, and he always looked forward to his bubble bath (where I allowed him to play with his toys.) He was a wonderful child! When I praised him for being so good, he said he liked being with me, and he didn't want to go to different homes every night.

I never had a problem getting Danny up in the morning so, after he was ready for bed, I let him watch his favorite TV program—ballet dancing. (He fell asleep in about ten minutes.)

Danny wasn't a picky eater; he especially liked strawberries. I often purchased them for him, and this sweet little boy would throw his arms around me to thank me. He appreciated everything I did for him. .

Danny was a real asset in my life. I loved him, and he showered me with his love. I think his mother was jealous of our affection for each other; she sent him to California to live with his dad. Although I asked her many times for his address, she never gave it to me.

Unfortunately, I've lost track of Danny. He would be over forty years old now. This five-year-old child actually did more for me than I did for him! I will never forget him, and I'm sure he has fond memories of the time he spent with me.

Regarding my neighborhood, it was unfortunate that other people were experiencing situations similar to the one that occurred with Danny and me. Since gangs were beginning to organize in the neighborhood, I didn't feel safe there anymore, so I reluctantly moved to another area of the city where I found a co-op I wanted to rent.

This was a twenty-story landmark building. It was located in a changing neighborhood, but I wanted to live there so I could spend my weekends assisting residents at the halfway house and teaching beginning reading to the adults.

My apartment was ideal for tutoring children. Unfortunately, Maureen, the woman who lived downstairs, kept complaining that she could hear the children running. The building was old, so sound traveled *at will* to other apartments. My floors were carpeted, so there wasn't too much I could do about her issue. We all tried to walk quietly, but she still complained. I really think she was lonely.

This matter was brought to the attention of the board. Since I was a board member, they were reluctant to do much about it. However, I invited them to check the carpeting in my apartment and make any recommendations they thought would be helpful to appease Maureen. I invited her to come along for the inspection, but she refused.

After the inspection, Maureen received a notification from the board indicating that my apartment was in compliance with all the regulations, so they were unable to make any recommendations for change. She was so provoked that she came to my door and yelled, "Why don't you go back to the convent where you belong!"

I stayed in my co-op for nine years. However, since the building was eighty years old, it needed new plumbing, new elevators, new heating systems, new lighting, new windows, new hall carpeting, and more. Our maintenance fees increased to the point where, unfortunately, I could no longer afford to live there. That's when I moved to Florida.

25
Chapter

FLORIDA: MY HOME

When I moved to Florida where my family lives, I found a villa in a "fifty-five-plus" community that is beautifully landscaped and well maintained. We have security at all three gates twenty-four hours per day. We also have many other amenities: three swimming pools, a fitness center, a library, and a game room. We also have choral groups, various classes/lectures, movies, and many clubs, including those for computer skills, carpentry, investments, gardening, knitting, and much more. We have tennis courts, basketball courts, and two golf courses. My neighbors are wonderful, and I am extremely happy here.

I decided I would like to resume substitute teaching. Since there are only a few children in our area, and the only Catholic school is about ten miles from my home, I applied for public school credentials. This experience was very rewarding, but again, I learned some rules the hard way.

Two very angry second-grade boys were fist-fighting in the cafeteria line. I separated them, putting one boy in the front of the line and the other at the end. That afternoon, I was called into the principal's office. She said I shouldn't have touched the boys! I asked her what I should have done, but her only recommendation was that I should not touch the children again. She certainly didn't solve my problem.

I wasn't quite sure what to do when little children ran up to hug me. Of course I wouldn't push them away, even though I knew I might be reprimanded for touching them.

Although I love teaching, I found the children much more difficult to discipline today. Even the little ones talked back to their teachers. When they were told to take *time out,* many of them refused to be isolated. There wasn't much anyone could do in those cases. My solution was to ignore the child for a little while and pretend that child wasn't there. Since no one likes to be ignored this seemed to work, and I didn't need to touch anyone.

My favorite class was pre-K. The children were so delightful! They were taught, among other things, to work nicely with one another, play games fairly, and be kind to each other. Their eyes sparkled with enthusiasm; they were innocent and trusting; they responded well to the love their teachers showered on them.

Unfortunately, when I was in their classroom one afternoon, I lost my balance and fell. I wasn't hurt, but the school administrators insisted that I fill out an accident report. The next thing I knew, I was called to the school board office and told I couldn't teach again until I saw a worker's comp doctor.

The doctor I saw was one of the nastiest people I have ever encountered. His first statement was, "This has nothing to do with your gender or your age." So I asked him why he brought it up. This was *not* a good start for my appointment!

I told him I wanted to return to the classroom until I had my surgery, which was scheduled for a month later. He refused this request. He said I was a hazard in the classroom, so I couldn't return until after I had my surgery and I could lift *fifty pounds*. Since I'd never been asked to lift even one pound, I was so disturbed and angry with his attitude that I told him to bring in a fifty-pound weight and I'd lift it right then and there. (I was furious enough that I probably could have done it.)

However, he said I was talking crazy, so now I had to see a neurologist before I returned to see him. He also said I'd need a Return to Work release from both my internist and surgeon, and these releases had to indicate I could life fifty pounds.

I called the school board and told Shirley, the coordinator for substitute teachers, what happened. She said, "The doctor overstepped his bounds." Teachers were asked to lift *twenty pounds* (not *fifty pounds*) in case of an emergency. She also said I didn't need to see a neurologist. She regretted that I couldn't return to school until after my surgery, but she couldn't override his directive for that issue. I was deeply disappointed with this decision.

After my surgery, I went to our fitness center and lifted a twenty-pound weight to prove to myself that I could lift it. Both my surgeon and internist gave me Return to Work forms, and at my word, they indicated I could lift a twenty-pound weight.

26
Chapter

RITA: ADDICTION COUNSELOR

Throughout the years, I have stayed in touch with Rita, my therapist from the rehab center. Although she isn't an alcoholic, she specializes in addictions. When I left the rehab, she agreed to counsel me privately. Since she didn't have any openings for me during the week, she actually saw me on Sunday mornings. Rita is very dedicated, and she practices *tough love*.

When I made my first visit to her office, she told me to keep a journal. I didn't do it, so when I arrived the next Sunday without it, she told me she had no time for people who didn't want to get well. If I wanted to leave, I could do it right then and there. I knew I needed help, and if I wanted Rita's assistance, I would need to cooperate with her and apply myself to my own recovery.

While I was in the convent, a good Sister learned to suppress her feelings—not show anger, happiness, depression, tiredness, sadness, or any other feeling. When Rita told me to write about my feelings, I didn't know how to do that, so I simply wrote my journal as a diary. I indicated all the things I'd done and places

I'd gone that week. Rita appreciated my effort, but she asked me to try writing about my *feelings*. Again, I had no idea how to do that since I didn't have any feelings. Due to subduing them for so many years, I didn't know *how* to feel.

She told me I was a robot, and I had lived in a cult. Although I never thought my convent life was a cult, this gave me food for thought. I didn't like hearing that I'd allowed superiors to change my persona to be the person *they* thought I should be. Rita finally convinced me that I had abnormal behavior due to the programing I lived with for thirty years. *Feelings* were not a part of my life.

I had a breakthrough the day I was a little late getting out to work. When I stepped into the elevator, I saw that our paperboy had pressed the buttons for all nineteen floors so he could stop and throw his papers in front of the correct apartments. I became angry and told him he shouldn't have done that. He cursed at me, and I "lost it." I started yelling at him, and by the time we arrived at the first floor, I was so furious that my whole body was shaking. (I have no idea why he didn't jump off the elevator when I started my tirade.)

When I saw Rita the next Sunday, she asked me how I was doing. I said, "Terrible!" When I told her what I'd done, she started smiling. I felt like my words were being changed from my mouth to her ears. Why would she smile when I had been so rude?

She told me she was excited because now she knew there was a flame in me that wasn't totally extinguished. I had finally started *feeling*! I have to admit I used my new feeling of anger to full capacity. I started showing anger at every little issue that arose. My friends said they didn't like the *new me*.

I was cautioned to temper my anger, but it was still a very good start for me. Little by little, Rita and I worked on developing other feelings. It was extremely painful, and it took many years.

Rita always made sure I was attending my AA recovery meetings, and that I had a good sponsor. She asked me what I learned at various meetings; she said I should always come away from them with something to think about. This is a practice I still maintain today.

Rita and I are still in contact. She's right there if I need her, and she still practices *tough love* today.

27
Chapter

TODAY'S SISTERS: MODERN AND TRADITIONAL LIFESTYLES

Diversity is the way nuns live today. Some nuns prefer to live in convents and wear their Habits; others have removed their Habits, and they work "in the world" in a variety of professional and community organizations.

Today, you may hear a Sister calling to another Sister, "Text me about that meeting," or, "Sister Jean would like to borrow your iPad." It was inconceivable to me that I'd ever hear such modern language in any Community.

However, in the sixties, Pope John XXIII wrote an encyclical (a document called *Vatican II)* that changed the lives of Sisters forever. He wanted nuns to look at the signs of the times and become more effective in their local communities.

Overnight, the structures of Community life disappeared. Most nuns no longer lived a rigid way of life.

Communities responded to the pope's document in various ways. Some quickly granted permission for their Sisters to begin re-forming their lifestyle, their clothing, and their living arrangements. These nuns were allowed to live and work among needy people. In this case, they could either wear their Habits or clothes that were appropriate for their community activities. For them, religious life became a balance of their work among God's people and their responsibilities to their Community.

Some conservative superiors responded by ordering their nuns to wear a knee-length Community uniform, along with a short veil. Other than this change in their dress, most of their old rules remained the same. There was obvious dissent in these Communities.

Today, just as their founders did, nuns work in areas where they contribute to everyday issues. They are nannies and youth ministers; they cook in restaurants that serve the poor; they are CEOs, and they are found in many other fields, such as technology development, broadcasting, social work, farming, ecology research, and more.

Some nuns were exhilarated by the pope's goal of bringing the Church into the modern world. Other nuns were devastated, and they had a hard time coming to terms with the reforms being enacted. To make matters worse for these nuns, the new document proclaimed that nuns were no more special to God than were good laypeople. However, all this unrest was a prelude to more serious matters to come.

The nuns who committed themselves to a modern lifestyle often had schedules that conflicted with their regular Community activities At times, they missed Community prayers. Sometimes they missed dinner, and they often had evening meetings with clients.

The nuns who preferred a traditional lifestyle wanted to be distinct. They still wear their Habits at all times. They have specific hours of prayer and a great respect for all the Community rules and regulations.

Following rituals is important to these Sisters: Mass, Habits, candles, incense, rosary, litanies, and changing their names. For them, rituals are meant to augment their worship and create an atmosphere of reverence. Wearing their Habit does not inhibit them from performing their duties as teachers, nurses, social workers, missionaries, daycare providers, and more.

Even the cloistered nuns responded to the pope's directives. (Most of these nuns lead a contemplative life that separates them from the world; the greatest part of their day is spent in prayer and silence.)

Besides maintaining their convent needs and prayer life, these nuns work in their own industries that sustain funds for their Community needs. They labor in their gardens, their laundries, and their bakeries. Their gift shops are filled with bakery goods, jam, pickled vegetables, greeting cards, and many types of arts and crafts,

After Vatican II, the life of many cloistered nuns changed dramatically. They continue their industries to maintain Community funds. However, now they have also found other ways to make their lives relevant to the world while maintaining their own prayerful way of life.

Many, **but not all**, of these contemplative nuns no longer live behind heavy grilles; they have opened their chapels to outsiders; they no longer wear heavy woolen garments during every season; they are counselors for those who wish to talk about their prayer life; some are allowed to leave their grounds to attend conferences related to contemplative living.

In all Communities, the Sisterhood of the past was very different from what new entrants to the religious life experienced. Young women lived and prayed together; diversity and uniqueness of individuals were recognized as assets. Rigid rules were no longer in vogue. There was no sign of blind obedience, and everyone's own personality was respected. However, many candidates were still conflicted about making a commitment to take vows in a religious Community. They wanted to show their love for God, but not necessarily as a nun. As laypersons they could still serve God and have a career and family, too.

When the winds of change reached the depths of religious Communities, there was a huge exodus of nuns who didn't like all the changes in the Church. They thought their religious Communities were moving too fast. They liked the old rules, and they showed stiff resistance to changing them. Even though the pope asked Communities to "open their windows" and see where they were needed outside their walls, there was no evidence that these nuns wanted to conform to such a directive.

Other Sisters left their Community because they got caught up in the essence of the Women's Liberation Movement. They were searching for equality and freedom from repression –issues that weren't found in their Communities.

Most Communities are now encountering serious difficulties because of their failing membership. At one time, there were as many as forty women entering the novitiate twice yearly. Now there are usually only three or four entrants each year. Many Sisters have retired or are disabled. Many are deceased. Over 60 percent of present-day Sisters are over the age of sixty-five. It is of great concern that Communities are dwindling so quickly. Rather than disintegrate, many Communities have merged with others.

Vatican II raised many issues, especially those of Sisters who work in the modern world and those who prefer a traditional lifestyle where living together in a convent is an important commitment for them. There is still tension in many Communities regarding traditional and modern ways of living. This is not a conflict between those who are faithful to traditions and those who have succumbed to the modern world. It is simply a difference in the way two groups understand how to carry forth the message of the Vatican Council.

For American nuns, *Vatican II* brought both freedoms and controversies that are still playing out today. However, whether today's Sisters prefer to live a traditional Community lifestyle, or they have changed their Habits to work in the world, Sisters have not lost view of their religious purpose. They maintain their vows of poverty, chastity, and obedience while living their lives in imitation of Jesus. In one of Matthew's gospels, he summed up the missions of today's nuns: feed the hungry, clothe the naked, give the thirsty something to drink, assist the sick and those in prison, and look after people you don't know. (Matthew 25:31-46)

28
Chapter

A POSSIBLE DREAM

When I entered the Community, I wanted to change the world. I said, "Yes" to a life devoted to God. I considered my consecration to God a lifetime position. However, as the world changed, I felt compelled to change with it.

Do I regret my years in the Community? No! But I regret that, while many of our Community decision-makers were open to the pope's directives, others were reluctant to help bring the Church into the modern world. These nuns were more comfortable living their lifestyle with the old rules. However, even our foundress worked among the people in any capacity where she was needed.

This was exactly what the pope declared nuns should do now...work in any capacity where they were needed: neighborhoods, communities, the business world, inner cities, nonprofit organizations, and any other places where they could be of service. I was elated! Religious women would finally become more relevant in the Church.

I was privileged that my Community allowed me to live and

work among the people for several years! I was extremely happy! I felt very close to God! I was following God's Call! I was living a *possible dream!*

However, when the permission for this lifestyle was withdrawn, and I was expected to return to the rigid rules of convent living, I could not bring myself to do what I was told without question. Since I rebelled against this mandate, I was given a choice: either submit to this directive, or take steps to sever my relations with the Community. Although my choice was difficult, I knew if I stayed in the Community I would become bitter, unhappy, frustrated, and unfulfilled.

Today, my Community is one of the most progressive religious organizations in the Church. They serve God's people wherever they're needed according to their gifts and talents. Although I severed my relations with them, my religious experiences will always stay with me. My life of service provided many spiritual and meaningful opportunities to be with God's people, especially through teaching and community service.

There are many paths to God. My Community was one path; now I follow another. I once had the willingness to devote my life to God's service as a nun. I still desire to dedicate my life to Him, but now I work in different community capacities. I have become a catalyst for hope, joy, and love with my involvement in my church and neighborhood activities. I know I don't need to be in a convent to do the work God puts in front of me. I can do that wherever I go.

I no longer need to practice blind obedience, and I no longer need to be the person others want me to be. I know God loves me—just as I am.

With the help of God, I started on my new journey: trying to be relevant by bringing the Church into the modern world. I could fulfill my dreams of serving God's people in their needs. My *possible dream* was finally a reality.

Glossary of Terms

Band   postulants who arrived on the same day and embarked on their novitiate journey together

blind obedience   performing without question whatever a superior commanded

collation   a snack where nuns could have a small repast

convent   living space of women religious

custody of the eyes   a rule that required eyes to be lowered at most times, especially during Profound Silence

discernment   a process of prayerful reflection that led a person to an understanding of God's Call

dowry   a prescribed amount of money that a new entrant brought to the Community to symbolize her desire to become a Bride of Christ. This money was used for her support and belonged to the Community after her profession of vows.

employment   task

exclaustration   a two-year period of prayer and discernment for a nun with perpetual vows who lived apart from the Community to decide whether she wanted to return to the Community or sever her relations definitively

formation   the physical and spiritual development of postulants and novices who were preparing for their profession of vows

Habit   a distinctive uniform worn by members of religious Communities that identified their Congregation

mission   assigned place of teaching or other position

motherhouse   main convent of a religious Community where the novitiate and infirmary were located, and where older Sisters lived after their retirement

novice   a candidate who spent a two-year period preparing to take her vows. A white veil was worn to indicate she was in training.

- **first-year novice:** a Sister who devoted this year to prayer and humble work

- **second-year novice:** Besides her regular schedule of prayer and spirituality, this Sister spent the major part of the year dedicated to her classes.

novice assistant	a novice who assisted new postulants to adapt to their surroundings and explain rules to them
novice mistress	a Sister in charge of religious formation of novices
novitiate	a separate part of the motherhouse set aside for novices' religious formation in preparation for taking their first vows
Office	a book of Latin psalms chanted mornings and evenings
postulant	an applicant who followed a six-month probation period
postulant mistress	a sister in charge of the religious formation of new entrants
prie-dieu	a bench and kneeler used in chapels and churches
professed Sisters	Sisters who took vows to deepen their commitment to God
Profound Silence	strictly maintained silence and custody of the eyes
refectory	dining room
reparation	penance for infraction of the rules
scullery	kitchen area where very large pots and pans were scrubbed by novices after each meal

Sister/nun	titles representing separate categories of religious women; in many cases, the titles are used interchangeably.
Transition Day	a ceremonial day when postulants received their Holy Habits and became formally admitted to the Community. It was considered their wedding day, so they wore wedding gowns to symbolize they were Brides of Christ. On this same day, some Sisters professed their first vows while others renewed their vows for various periods of time.
Vows	a solemn public promise made to God where a Sister deliberately and freely committed herself to practice poverty, chastity, and obedience

- **poverty:** a pledge to give all personal possessions to the Community and trust the Community would allocate money to provide for her physical and spiritual needs

- **chastity:** a voluntary vow to abstain from all forms of sexual activity. It is the quality of being pure, modest, and celibate.

- **obedience:** a full surrender of one's will to follow superiors' directives

CPSIA information can be obtained
at www.ICGtesting.com
Printed in the USA
LVHW082357180521
687839LV00012B/782